Taking a Long Road Home

Taking a Long Road Home

A Memoir

EUGENE C. BIANCHI

For Don Frilson
with very best
wishes —

— Gene
12-21-10

RESOURCE *Publications* · Eugene, Oregon

TAKING A LONG ROAD HOME
A Memoir

Resource Publications
An Imprint of Wipf and Stock Publishers
199 W. 8th Ave., Suite 3
Eugene, OR 97401
www.wipfandstock.com

ISBN 13: 978-1-60899-788-6

Manufactured in the U.S.A.

Se tu segui tua stella,
non puoi fallire a glorioso porto.

If you follow your star,
you cannot miss the splendid harbor.

—DANTE ALIGHIERI, *INFERNO* 15:55–56

Contents

Acknowledgments

I OWE A DEBT of gratitude to many, starting with the Heilbrun Fellowship program at Emory University. The Heilbrun funds retired professors who are completing research and writing in their areas of interest.

Thank you to John Loudon for your careful editing and candid suggestions; to Robert R. Rahl for your technical and substantive work in shaping this memoir; and to my wife, Peggy Herrman. Peggy encouraged me all along the way. She provided both professional criticism and good judgment about sensitive issues.

Finally, I am thankful to everyone who in overt and subtle ways contributed to my growth in knowledge and a little wisdom. Many people appear in this memoir. It has been a pleasure to recall their faces and voices. There is also a much wider assembly of those who deserve my thanks for being part of my life in usually unseen ways. This is the thrust of a Lakota prayer of gratitude "for all my relations," that is, all those who are part of me:

> I pray for all my relations . . .
> All those who walk, crawl, fly, and swim,
> Seen and unseen,
> To the good spirits that exist in every part of Creation.

Introduction

*It's odd that after thousands of years of great spiritual example
and literature we have to remind ourselves that spirituality
is to be found in everyday life.*

—THOMAS MOORE

NOT LONG AGO, THE Provost of Emory University, where I taught for four decades, asked me what I planned to do after retirement. I told him I had only one open slot on my resume, to become a saint. This was something of a conversation stopper. After moments of silence and a puzzled look, he said: "You mean a canonized saint as in the Catholic Church?" I said no, that I had a different view of sanctity than the canonizing process. I was referring to a less heroic notion of holiness. I meant something simpler: to move beyond or beneath religious institutions and their teachings.

I wanted to reconnect with a natural or primordial way of living spirit in the ups and downs of everyday life. My path has been a lifelong search for home, a true way for body/spirit here and now. Some may see this as just secular living. I've come to view daily existence as the main arena of spiritual life. Other aspects of traditional religion can be helpful but are secondary. To get to this gut-level, down-home spirit in the quotidian, I've had to let go of heady theories and false estimates of myself to learn from hard times. Without becoming a Pollyanna, I seek to discover divinity in persons and nature. How might we re-imagine life, secular and spiritual, intimately linked to one another?

In this memoir I try to explain myself to myself. I invite readers to look over my shoulder as I select events over seven decades. My bag of mixed motives for this venture surely includes a quotient of ego and another of self-deception. Yet that's all part of being human. If we had to exclude every trace of self-interest, we'd never write anything personal. And I dare to hope that you may resonate with some of my experiences.

I've been involved with religion as a Jesuit priest and later as a university professor. I want to trace changes in my personal grasp of it. I continue to be interested in specific spiritual traditions, especially their contemplative sides. As a teacher and writer, I've spent a lot of time reflecting on church reform. My outlook has become increasingly ecumenical. While the contemplative path is paramount for me, religious institutions remain important, because they influence the world for good or ill.

I hope my tale will strike some sparks with the ever-increasing number of "in-between" people who have one foot, however tentatively, in a tradition and the other searching for new spiritual paths. Being in-between will surely expand in a cybernetic age. Science and technology are moving too fast for it to be otherwise.

My approach to the spiritual did not come as a sudden vision. It fell together gradually, a piece here, a stone there. It dawned on me in quiet ways through a lifetime of study, but especially during times of emotional turmoil. It's a story of discovery that extends from a childhood with Italian immigrants to the Jesuits to being a leading advocate for married priests to finding the spiritual in the everyday. It's a circuitous journey that may resonate with others whose lives and longings parallel mine in some way.

Since I write as an elder, I will be interpreting things from a distance. But approximations to how it was in Oakland, California in the forties or in the Jesuit order are good enough. I may have a better chance to see the wider pattern from a longer vista. I've also had the good fortune of keeping written journals from the late fifties to bring back specific memories.

My vocation as a teacher is another reason for writing this memoir. I've always said to students that they didn't have to accept my viewpoints. I hope the book will stimulate reflection in readers who feel kinship and in those who don't.

1

Wine-Making in a Dirt Floor Basement

*Life can only be understood backwards
but must be lived forwards.*

—Søren Kierkegaard

DRESSED IN MY SALT and pepper, uniform corduroy pants, I came home from third grade at Sacred Heart School in Oakland to witness the inter-family wine-making event. A block away I could see the stained wooden grape boxes from my cousin's place in the country piled empty along the sidewalk. My heart leapt at the sight. I ran with my book bag swung over my navy cardigan sweater. Sister Claudine would not have approved my hanging around with Italian immigrant forebears sipping last year's Dago Red from stubby, chiseled glasses in the dirt floor basement of my grandfather's house. But I was now beyond the border of rules.

The old men were bragging about last year's vintage as their rubber boots stomped the fresh grapes in large wood tubs. Then they poured the dark brew into a manually operated crusher. The pungent smell is still vivid. The old guys outdid each other with stories in *Genovese* dialect, some from the old country, others from their experiences in America. The place reeked of crushed grapes, the latter used by a few brave souls to produce *grappa*, a distilled liquor made from remains of the winepress. My uncle John's amateur radio system strung with thrown-away speakers crisscrossed the basement, supplying background music from hit tunes of the twenties and thirties. But the music was poor competition for the voices urging on the two men who turned the screw of the

1

crusher round and round like figures from a Bruegel painting of harvest time.

No one begins life with a clean slate, a *tabula rasa*. Only later, of course, did I realize how immersed I was in an ethnic Italian-American culture. Even they were not generic Italians, but *paisani*, neighbors, from the countryside in Liguria and Tuscany with their specific habits. On that wine-making day, I would never have thought that someday I would come back to this basement to find clues for authentic living. As an eight-year-old altar boy, I assigned religion and God to the Holy Names nuns who taught me. They were mostly Irish women who bespoke discipline in their long black robes and starched white coifs that hid their hair and foreheads. I took it for granted that someone so specially attired was also special to God. For me the spiritual realm was connected with convent corridors that I waxed and the dark high wainscoting topped by somber portraits of mothers superior long gone.

Religion had to do with the priest house and serving Mass in black cassock and white surplice, carrying wine and water for the great ritual, ringing the little bell for the *Sanctus* and the consecration of the host, as well as the Latin prayers: *Introibo ad altare Dei . . . (I will go in to the altar of God . . .)*. It had to do with the sacristy where priests put on liturgical garments. It had to do especially with the confessional with its heavy drapery and sliding door and recitation of sins and dark pews on Saturday afternoon where we said our three Our Fathers and three Hail Marys in reparation for the week's sins. Such formal confession was a prerequisite for receiving communion on Sunday.

These aspects of a Catholic childhood enfolded the context of my early life, but they were not its deepest roots. That dirt basement and the key players around it on 42nd Street in Oakland, California really formed me. Gertrude Stein spoke of Oakland as a place with "no there there," but for me it had great on-the-ground salience or "thereness." My maternal grandparents lived right across the street from us. Luigia Mangini, my *Nonna*, an intellectual of sorts, stretched her limited formal education to read the Italian newspaper every day with her Woolworth reading glasses. In her big wedding picture, she was strong and quite good looking, wearing a wool sepia dress sitting next to *Nonno*, my grandfather, in dark serge with a heavy mustache. Of course, that's a later judgment of her looks. In childhood I was more interested in her cooking and banter as she held forth on everything. I provided an audience for her. *Nonna* was opinionated. She hated Roosevelt for opposing Mussolini and getting us into World War II, but she gradually developed more tolerance toward Eisenhower whose name she pronounced "Ouzenhourah." At her heavy, wooden kitchen table, where family life took place near a wood-burning stove, I learned by a kind of osmosis that reading was important. Of course, she never lectured on the value of reading. That came indirectly through the feel and smell of pasta dough that she would powder and roll and toss and roll again.

That table was important because there I watched her make from scratch the world's best ravioli, which I looked forward to eating with the abandon of youth. The smell of her mushroom sauce simmering in that small kitchen is still with me. *Nonna's* house was also a main comfort zone when the *Sturm und Drang* of my own home across the street became overwhelming. *Nonna* went to church, but expressed independent judgment about clerical foibles. She voiced a more benign judgment, for example, of my second grade teacher, Sister Anne Marie, who ran off with a mechanic, a scandal of cosmic proportions in 1938. "The poor thing was unhappy in that dark building," she would say in *Genovese*. I remember holding my grandmother's hand on the way to semi-annual Italian missions (intense preaching events with loud off-key congregational singing of *Noi vogliam Dio, chènostro Padre* "We want God who is our Father"*)* at nearby churches. On the way home we would collect mushrooms in empty lots and gather eucalyptus pods whose scent was thought to ward off bedroom varmints. I remember her, pitchfork in hand, turning the soil to plant vegetables. And I see her in a long brown overcoat with fur collar holding a large purse with both hands in front of her. As an altar boy, I saw this classic country immigrant stance replicated many times.

John Mangini, my uncle, who never left home (except for a stint in the army during the "good war"), contributed more to me than I ever realized in youth. In addition to his tinkering with old radio parts and stringing speakers around the property and messing with old cars, he was a professional house painter. He was tall and well built with straight hair that he kept dyed dark all his life. The color depended on which drug store product he was using at the time. Italians have the strangest nicknames. Some people referred to him as John or Gianni, but for the most part, he was "Cooka." The provenance of that one remains a mystery. But he, too, was a master of nicknames. When I would flee the familial turmoil at home for the saner clime across the street, he would ask me what "Lucca" or "*Il Re di Lucca*" (the King of Lucca) or "GinoBianchiGino" was up to in the zone of fury. And he had his secret nicknames, known only to his special initiates, such as "Gambing" ("short legs" with accent on "bing") for a friend's wife on the block. Cooka was complex and simple at once. Never an academic performer, he didn't finish high school. Most everybody liked him, but people would speak to him as though talking to a child or a simpleton with that special inflection in their voices. He was generous to a fault, sending money from his meager resources to questionable religious charities, a habit I could not talk him out of, even in my heady Jesuit days.

Cooka built his own chapel in the chicken house that had been part of our Victory Garden during the war. His shrine consisted of holy pictures, rosaries and other religious memorabilia placed in wooden niches. Cooka had recurrent nervous breakdowns, the biggest happening in 1943 at Camp Carson in Colorado. It eventually got him discharged from the army. I recall the day in 1942 when the family walked him to the nearby Santa Fe station to return to Camp Carson, while Carling, one of the elder wine-makers, was showing him how to crouch behind boulders to avoid bullets. Hardly the remedy for his nervousness.

As a younger man, he was racked with scruples, a condition exacerbated by the sin-guilt mentality he encountered at our parish church. After painting a hall for the Italian Catholic Federation, for example, he would crucify himself with worries about leaving lights on because this might cause a fire. His "Chapel of the Gallinah" (Genoese version of "Chapel of the Chicken House"), as I called it, seemed to serve as his place of worship when he no longer went to Mass. Cooka had an explosive side, ranting on about those sons-of-a-bitch priests and nuns who, he thought, scared him into scruples as a child. Like Dante talking with Virgil, he would assign special torments and places in hell to these religious professionals. Such tirades, often with a touch of humor, usually took place around the old well, dug by my grandfather. We would sit on an equally ancient bench behind the iron pump handle, as we looked out on fava beans, onions, potatoes, and apricot trees. Of course, he would recognize one or other kindly priest or nun who attempted to assuage his scruples. Father Varni was okay. In a quiet voice, this priest would say, "John, don't worry about those things. They're not sins." Cooka replaced visits to church with private devotions at some Native American burial grounds along the bay. He felt strongly about honoring these bones. Stray cats became part of his community. He couldn't deny them the benevolence of food and some shelter, despite the hygienic mess that two dozen felines made.

I was unconsciously learning a lot just being with my uncle. Without explicit language, he was teaching me about the brokenness of life. It was a slow immersion in the limits of our desires and of life in general. I was letting Cooka's pain and sadness seep into me over time. He was helping me grow into the *lacrimae rerum*, the tears of existence. I didn't realize it then, but I, as the son he never had, was receiving Cooka's tenderness despite his dirty overalls and unshaven face. I was giving him a chance to be fatherly. He developed a term of endearment for me, "Putiti," when I came into view. He would often turn "Putiti" into a chant of repetition. I don't know how he conjured up "Putiti," but it might have been from sounds I made as a toddler. He called my brother, George, "Tofoleti." This derived from a childhood incident concerning slippers (*pantofola*).

When he had some money, he would buy me gifts such as my first electric train. This was during the Depression. He first walked me to the nearby hardware store to see if I liked it. He was proud of his work as a house painter and would regale me with stories about the elegant homes he painted in Oakland and Berkeley. He was particularly proud of his abilities with gum finish, a glossy protective coating on woodwork. In the late forties, I accompanied him to Fresno in a Santa Fe (he pronounced "Fee") steam-driven train to an Italian Catholic Federation meeting where he proudly played the clarinet in a marching band. In his better moods, he would bang out John Philip Souza on his harmonica with great gusto.

Another poignant phase of Cooka's life was his longing for a woman. Yet his neurotic, depression-oriented personality and his child-like simplicity kept him tied to his parents. His tastes in women were certainly integrated long before that would have been common in a working class area that saw substantial white flight after the World War II. His pin-ups were frequently African American women. When I pointed out his spirit of "integration," it wasn't hard to detect his frustrated desire. It may be that out of his pain around scruples and loneliness, he was able to develop an amazing kindness of spirit toward me and my younger brother. Cooka might be fulminating against those no-good Italians who abandoned the neighborhood, his right fist pounding into his left hand, but I could always detect a note of humor in the recitation. He would sentence the runaways to hanging and end the soliloquy with a loud "pong!" as the trap door sprung. However crazy *Barba* (dialect term for uncle) *Gianni* might have been, his nephews felt at ease around him, enjoyed being with him, sensing that they had his unconditional acceptance.

Antonio "Tony" Mangini, my maternal grandfather, *Nonno*, was already an older person when I was a child. He was relatively short and wiry with a handlebar mustache and a mellow personality. *Nonno* didn't say much, even in the hurly-burly of wine making, although his English was somewhat better than *Nonna's*, which was virtually non-existent. She could live surrounded by *paisani* who spoke either dialect or regular Italian. I remember three tableaus of *Nonno*. The first is that of my grandfather on an old bicycle (he eventually traded up by using my discarded bike) riding down to Emeryville and returning up 42nd Street, walking the bike with a large load of long thin oak castoff strips from a lumber mill poised precariously—so it seemed to me—over the handle bars and the seat. The bundle was always tied with old strips of cloth from discarded clothing. He came to the area in 1895 taking a job picking strawberries near Half Moon Bay. *Nonno* saved money and started a horse-drawn garbage business with a *paisano* in Oakland in the first decade of the last century. He was tying up the horses one day when he spotted my grandmother in a relative's yard. *Nonna* said that he leapt over the fence to present himself. I may have inherited some of his venturing spirit in a number of life decisions.

A second picture of my grandfather is of him sitting in the doorway of his dirt basement, using natural light to guide his hatchet into the kindling wood he had carted home. He seemed to always wear the same outfit: black denim pants hitched up by thick suspenders over a long sleeve, faded blue work shirt. I would appear on Saturdays to beg a dime for a movie. He would sink the hatchet in the chopping block and dig into a front pocket for a deep leather purse with silver fastener. Cooka, who stood over six feet, used to criticize the old man for not digging a deeper opening to the basement, especially after my uncle banged his head on the low top. That gave rise to a commentary on his parents' frugal ways, "not wanting to spend another God-damn nickel on things." Yet it was precisely this frugality that allowed *Nonno* to save enough to build not only his own house, but also our house and a four unit apartment adjacent to it. One had to have "cashy" in those days. It wasn't easy for an immigrant, who started his own garbage business with horse and wagon, to persuade bankers to make loans. But I could also sympathize with Cooka when I, too, bumped my head on the low opening.

The third tableau of *Nonno* is especially memorable since I would become a priest and teacher of religion. After retiring at age sixty, he spent the next thirty years as a vegetable grower to our neighborhood. In friends' empty lots, he cultivated row on row of beans, tomatoes, lettuce, onions, Swiss chard and all manner of other ingredients that went into Mediterranean cooking. Walking to school, I could see him going meticulously from plant to plant holding a long pole with a watering can at the far end. When he could, he pumped the water from a well into a large container and scooped it into manageable buckets that he toted to the end of rows where he had dug irrigation ditches. He sold the produce informally for very little, or he would give it away. During the Depression, his vegetables kept food on our table when my father was out of work for years. *Nonno's* last regular job was in a linoleum factory where the fumes made him sick. He retired in 1930, the year of my birth. Getting outdoors was healing for him and it brought him back to his roots in the earth of Fontanarossa, a small mountain town outside of Genoa. I made a pilgrimage there years later to scout out the humble ruins of what was called "*u bosco,*" the grove, where he was born in 1870, the year of Italy's unification. I stood by the grave of his own grandfather and looked up toward the terraced produce gardens and fruit trees. Closeness to the soil and its fruitfulness were his real religion.

Of course, as a somewhat pious young boy, I didn't understand this. One day on my way home from school, a walk of only three blocks, I stopped off at one of his lots. He was taking a break, sitting by the hand pump and chewing some kind of foul-smelling Italian tobacco that produced ghastly brown spit and turned teeth maroon. I asked him why he didn't go to church, except on Christmas or Easter. I must have been worried about the salvation of his soul, since the nuns and priests insisted on us attending Sunday Mass under pain of mortal sin for which we could go to hell forever. And I remembered vividly how Monsignor Sampson at high Mass on Christmas, striding to the communion rail, his huge gray-topped head and deep-set eyes trembling, would berate men like my grandfather standing in their one good suit of clothes at the rear of the church. Why, he thundered, did they come to church so rarely?

Didn't they realize that the Baby Jesus came down for them? How could they reject him by not going to Mass? He insisted that they come every Sunday. Perhaps, I thought, these *contadini* with limited education just didn't understand the Monsignor's English with an Irish brogue. Back at the lot, *Nonno* spat, chuckled and looked up at me. "Jewjing," (that's how he pronounced "Eugene"), he said, "*sono cattolico e religioso ma non sono fanatico*." (I'm Catholic and religious, but I'm not a fanatic.)

When he said he was a Catholic, he claimed allegiance to his Italian culture, steeped in centuries of religious monuments, rituals and sensibilities. His use of the word "religious" pointed to an honest way of living, an ethical life style, that all religious traditions encourage. Perhaps my father, the notorious Natale Gino Bianchi, summed up this dimension in his own quaint way when I would ask him about confessing his sins to a priest. He would pause with a look of amazement on his pinkish, round face. Why did he need to go to confession? Then he would proclaim his oft repeated response: "I haven't killed anybody. I haven't robbed anyone. I haven't done anything wrong." (Of course, he was oblivious of his treatment of our mother.) As far as *Nonno* and Pa were concerned, they were living decent, ethical lives and saw no need to follow the confessional habits of women and children. If the latter wanted to recite peccadillos through the sliding door of the confessional, it was just the way of priest-ridden women and the kids they coerced into the discipline. If the practice kept wives in good humor and held the children in line, all the better. One could claim that the men were just lazy regarding religious duties. But when they saw themselves as not "fanatics," they were saying something important. What counted were the hard daily realities of putting bread on the table and treating others decently in the process. It was the gritty theology of working class Italian men transferred to the new world. Involving themselves in many church rituals seemed fanatical. If God were to be found, it would have to be in the daily rounds.

Freudians sometimes refer to the interactions of parents and children as the family romance, surely an ironic term given the interplay between our common idea of romance and the dramatics of real families. And Tolstoy, hardly a paragon of familial success, said that all good families are good in the same way, while bad family relationships are bad in their own peculiar modes. As I think about the house at number 933 on 42nd Street, I find both Freud and Tolstoy pertinent. The Bianchi household evidenced no perceptible romance between husband and wife, and it was a "bad" marital environment in its own peculiar ways. I place "bad" in quotes because a relationship between father, mother and two sons over decades is too complex to be characterized as simply bad. We have to look at positive aspects, too. But on the whole, our family interactions would never qualify for a Dr. Phil manual of the successful unit.

Yet out of this textbook case of wrong moves came two reasonably healthy sons, each carrying his own wounds from childhood in different ways. Without trying to answer the underlying problem of genetics and environment, we can agree on the mutual influence of nature and nurture. Even the experts haven't figured out the intricacies of this interplay. Perhaps the best way to get a fix on my family milieu is to look at the older actors first and then the responses of my brother and me.

Natale Gino Bianchi, after forty-four months (that's how he always started when telling war stories following ample wine and food) in the Italian field artillery during World War I, migrated by rapid stages to Oakland. In the retreat from Caporetto, made famous for English readers by Hemingway in *A Farewell To Arms*, my father said that he rode two horses to death trying to escape. He would point to a scar on his forehead where a bullet grazed him while he was sleeping against a tree. Like other immigrants, he had family relations in the Bay Area, mainly his older sister, Cesira. Gino was a terror to live with . . . not all the time, but most of the time. He was built like a small silo with a round face and ruddy complexion. When I later met his brother, Giorgio, in Italy, I recognized the body type.

My brother and I inherited the lankier physical shape of my mother's family, although George's disposition was closer to Gino's. "You're just like your father," Ma used to say to George when he displeased her. It's interesting how good and bad roles, repeatedly prescribed by parents, become durable markers of personality. We tend to live up to these given roles. Even later when George became a lawyer and president of the Hibernia Bank in San Francisco, my mother could not give up the habit of comparing her sons negatively to the good boys in the neighborhood. She was very short on any compliments to us, except when we were "very, very good." She might say this only when we conformed to the ways of those she esteemed as paragons of goodness. In my mother's convoluted mind, such negative sketching was a kind of humility, lest in the classical Greek sense, the gods strike us down for hubris. But it was also an extension of her own need to be a victim. Victims are not supposed to win or boast about winning.

Life with Gino in a frame, four room house, was frequently nerve-racking and sometimes hellish. He was a bundle of easily ignited fury. In later years, George and I engaged in what we called "shrinkology," speculating about "the citizen's" (George's nickname for Gino who proudly became a naturalized U.S. citizen) early formation in the rural village of Tofori outside of Lucca. Did his over-burdened (eleven children) mother have no time for him in the dawn to dusk work routine of tenant farmers? Did the long stint in World War I brutalize him? Did he just learn among peers that straightforward bullying worked? There was nothing indirect or passive-aggressive about Gino. He was pure in-your-face aggression. He didn't sulk for hours or days building up a temper tantrum. Provocations brought immediate responses. At least we didn't have to hold our breath in anticipation. I feared him in his bad moods, but also saw him as a pillar of security. He made a living for us and would defend us when necessary. When a grammar school boy and his brother jumped me on the way home from school, Gino lost no time knocking on that family's door with tough talk.

The chief catalyst for his explosions around dinner time (and we always ate well, thanks in part to *Nonno's* vegetable gardens) was the volatile mixture of my mother's highly-developed victimhood and Gino's well-honed talent for victimizing. I remember so many episodes in which subtle and overt exchanges lit the fuse. He would come home from work as a welder in federal navy yards carrying his black metal lunch pail. After washing his face, he would emerge into the kitchen area. The radio on top of the refrigerator declared the nightly news. Gino was a news junkie, something I carried on. My mother, Katie or "Chieti" in more ethnic circles, had prepared dinner and was ironing clothes on a pull-down ironing board. I was seated at the swirled green Formica table with silver, pipe-like legs, an art deco standard of the thirties and forties. I was very hungry after playing in the school yard, and the smell of an Italian fish or meat stew was killing me. But I could sense a major blow-up about to happen.

Katie would recite some incident of the day as she pressed down on the ironing board: she met Gloria Perucchi at the grocery store and learned that her family was moving to a "high-tone" district in the hills, or that Mr. Backus, the old bachelor down the street, spoke so kindly to her, never raising his voice when she retrieved the ball I had thrown into his yard. Backus was such a dear elder to her, a true saint. I could see the smoke curling up from Gino's ears. If that didn't ignite the fuse, ma would go on to say that Margie was on the verge of a nervous breakdown because Mill was so insensitive to her, or that Cooka was drinking too much and yelling at her because she told him he looked like a bum in his unwashed overalls, or that Jack Bozzini was so nice to his wife when she wanted to go to church or play cards during the day with Maria Ferretti. Whatever it was, she knew just how to pull the trigger. Her verbal moves were low-keyed, but the undertone was that of the martyr entering the Coliseum. I think he picked up on that tone, even more than the content of the incidents, although they, too, were freighted with tempting morsels. He heard the sound that had a self-pitying ring about it. Gino was an unconscious Nietzschean in his dislike of pity and, especially, self-pity. One of his favorite summary lines about Katie was: "You muddah want pity, pity, pity (pronounced 'peetee')."

But with that lead-in, the *Übermensch* was off to the races. As his voice escalated in Italian and broken English, Katie would break in with "O, Gino, don't get mad, don't get mad." Of course, these pleas would only make him madder. Weekends were the worse times because Gino would pull whiskey from the cooler in the pantry. In that oversimplified distinction between sleepy drunks and mean drunks, he was clearly the latter. The bottle accentuated his demons. In part, he may have been disappointed by having to take charity, as it were, from his in-laws when he was out of work in the 1930s. When his job in the Vallejo navy yard was secure after the war, he wanted to move there to strike out on his own. But Katie didn't want to leave her familiar environment and prevailed on him not to buy a house in Vallejo. How much did he resent her for keeping him tied to her parents? In the trade-offs of life, I probably benefited greatly by not moving to Vallejo.

My reactions to the kitchen incidents were to eat and run. Although I felt the misery of it, which probably contributed to nervous anxiety throughout my life, my basic response mechanism was avoidance. Sometimes I could not get out of harm's way when I had done some misdeed that summoned Gino's anger. Although he didn't hit us often, it was very scary when he did. Usually he would resort to loud threats, but when I think back on it, I don't recall him putting us down psychologically. With him it was direct force. He didn't have the verbal ability to critique us with the mental indirections of my mother. At any rate, my avoidance techniques tended to be of two kinds: mental and physical. During a kitchen confrontation, I would pull away emotionally and stay quiet, or I would try to change the subject, which usually was as successful as stopping a gale by raising my hand.

I wonder how much this emotional avoidance negatively affected my later life. It was a pretty good survival technique in childhood, but the pattern was not good for listening to the feelings of others, especially my future wives. This is most likely also connected to what psychologists call "perseveration" (a lack of attention to the conversation at hand) that others notice in me. On the contrary, George, who spent more time than I did at home (I escaped into the Jesuits after high school) had inherited much of Gino's disposition. He would confront him, even if it meant being chased around the kitchen table. George, though psychologically quite subtle, has always been more direct and emotionally vulnerable than I. In him, Gino would meet Gino. George and I have speculated on how Gino would have done with a wife who stood up for herself. Such are the imponderable what-ifs that present themselves, but offer no real answers.

My second mode of avoidance was to just get away from the family romance. When things got hot, I could walk across the street to my grandparents' house. The blessings of extended kinship brought calming acceptance. *Barba Gianni* would get me laughing with his antics. Or I could regroup with other kids. There was the peaceful house of Ted Cantino who became a physician or the interesting house of Robert Moran who owned armies of toy soldiers, and where later I heard Churchill give his Iron Curtain speech. And then there was always the school playground at Sacred Heart for a game of stick ball. I was becoming a master of avoidance.

But there was an upbeat side to the drama. Beyond all the craziness, and there was too much of it, Katie and Gino, both considerably flawed, were good enough parents. In the traditional division of labor between husband and wife, my mother elicited one of her few positive statements about Gino: "Your father is a good provider." Since marriage was largely about survival, especially during the Depression, such a compliment was notable. Religion, social convention and limited finances conspired to keep unhappy marriages together. So Katie, who subtly played into Gino's raging, would never leave him, however threatening his anger.

Such was the mutual compact of the family romance in many households. Yet from a child's perspective this less than perfect scene had its merits. It provided a stable base from which I could maneuver to deal with the madness. There was security and food on the table. There was predictability and a refuge across the street. I always felt an abiding love from my mother despite her annoying traits of self-pitying manipulation. I'm sure I got lots of that benevolence from her long before I could remember it.

Gino was not always a raging bull. I remember him taking me by the hand for walks in the neighborhood. On one of these, I could hear radios from open windows blaring Joe Louis's knockout of Max Schmeling in 1936. I recall family outings in Mosswood Park where partial truces were honored on a Sunday afternoon. Gino's weekend bingeing was confined to Friday and Saturday nights. Remember, he was a good provider and had to go to work early on Monday. Occasionally, he would take me to a downtown movie theatre and buy me ice cream on the long walk back. He taught us by example the values of hard work, sacrifice, delayed gratification and simple common sense. His frequently-voiced comment, "Dey don know what dey want," stands over against the later utopian aspirations of the hippie generation. Gino didn't learn to drive, so we never had a car. In his own way, he was proud of both sons, although he was not able to express affection.

Katie, despite her neuroses, was the main source of our stability. She provided a trustworthy ambience of mostly unconditional love. This was her true center beyond the histrionics. No doubt, her poor relations with Gino made her concentrate on George and me for emotional support. But even in a good marital relationship, her grounding presence to us would not have altered. Kids pick up on that trustworthy presence gathering them in without overwhelming them. They know they are loved without having to be constantly assured of it. This presence gave me a sense of stability. I never doubted that when I left for school with my mother talking about neighborhood news to my grandmother by the window in the kitchen, I would find her at home when I came back for lunch where she would spoil me with lamb chops and steamed fresh peas from my grandfather's garden. Another enduring trait was Katie's care for the less fortunate in our neighborhood. She would dispense food and good advice to single moms and frail shut-ins. More than this, they knew she cared about them.

While the world of 42nd Street provided my main understanding of what it meant to be human, Catholic school and parish inserted me into formal religion. As a kid, this consisted of church rituals directed by the nuns and priests. Then there was secular life as a realm apart. Everyone accepted this divide. Church professionals even promoted it. They set the rules for being favored in the eyes of God and worthy of heavenly rewards. Some of these codes tied in with being good Americans, but many of them had a special Catholic flavor. This was especially true about sex. From my first awakening to a girl named Rosemary in the sixth grade under the no-nonsense gaze of Sister Brendan, I was into a long struggle with dirty thoughts. Rosemary was very smart and she also had well-developed breasts for a pre-pubescent girl. It made me wonder about the well-covered but ample breasts of Sr. Brendan, who would have killed me if she had an inkling of my reveries.

Religious devotions dominated the Catholicism of the thirties and forties. Mass was a devout practice for most lay people who said the rosary while the priest with back turned to the congregation followed the Latin rite. Yet I remember a feeling of awe (when I wasn't too sleepy) while serving Mass with the priest genuflecting and raising the host. Other devotions were novenas, First Fridays and expositions of the Blessed Sacrament. These rites, together with slightly off-key singing by the choir, instilled in me an emotional sensitivity for the sacred. I still recall the affective impact of the three hours service on Good Friday with the stations of the cross combined with preaching about the seven last words of Christ. Now I would have to be chained to a pew to undergo the bad sermons and the lugubrious motions of Good Friday. My view of these practices has greatly changed over the years. But as a child I was unconsciously learning at an emotional level a sense of reverence for the transcendent.

The unbridgeable roles of priest and laity underscored the Catholicism of my youth. These differences mirrored the division between religion and life. The grace gained from the sacraments was supposed to help one in everyday life, but there was little sense that ordinary living itself was full of openings to grace. Religion was also separated from nature. Catholic theology held that grace built on nature. But priests presented earthly life as a vale of tears that we would escape in heaven. Nature, beautiful as it was, formed a backdrop and a set of metaphors for the really important thing: the salvation of individual souls in the afterlife. In this scheme, church rules gained great importance. Mortal sin, the road to hell, could result from breaching church mandates, such as missing Mass on Sunday, eating meat on Friday, not confessing to a priest once a year and receiving communion, not marrying in the church and not raising one's children as Catholics. The hierarchy claimed that people needed direction for their own spiritual benefit. Critics might counter that a religion of clerical rules was a convenient way of enhancing control. Yet I was oblivious of such critiques at Sacred Heart Parish.

Most sins for a growing boy revolved around sex. Here the physical and the spiritual were at war. We were told that everything having to do with sex was serious business. Missteps in this domain could land one in hell. I recall trying to not to look at sexy advertisements of women on bill boards and movie marquees during streetcar rides to high school in San Francisco. I probably had it pretty bad, as they say, but some were even more frightened by scruples about sex. It took me years to develop a sane mentality about masturbation and sexual thoughts. Later as a young Jesuit high school teacher, I remember walking out in disgust as Father Newport, famous for his ability to frighten students during school retreats, was graphically measuring how far boys could go in kissing and touching. He always concluded with the grim example of the boy who went too far and was plunged into hell after a car wreck on the way home from a dance. This was in the fifties, but by then I could see the absurdity of these still prevalent teachings.

Some of the lessons learned in the closed ranks of ethnic Catholicism gave me a religious starting point. Yet in our Catholic defensiveness, we overstated our importance in the eyes of God. I remember thinking it a sin to go into a Protestant church or participate in their services. After all, they had left the true church to follow heretical ways. Ours was the right way and all other creeds were erroneous, leading us away from God. What would later be called ecumenism was then presented as indifference. God was a Catholic who looked sternly on his children associating with those of other creeds. The church discouraged mixed marriages and obliged the faithful to raise their children as Catholics. In high school we heard lectures about the pitfalls of attending non-Catholic colleges.

So much in our lives is an accident of timing and place. Some claim a divine master plan working itself out, but I have come to see these events as adapting to life's contingencies. Aldo Bozzini, a year ahead of me at Sacred Heart grammar school, was awarded a scholarship to the Jesuit high school in San Francisco, St. Ignatius. This was an unusual destination for Oakland boys who gravitated to high schools on the East-Bay side. It was a long daily journey in the orange trains across the Bay Bridge and then by streetcar to SI. I emulated Aldo, a bright personality who would become an actor and director of plays with various day jobs to support him. Little did I know then that he was also gay and would spend much of his life in a stable partnership. Homosexuality was as foreign to us as the man in the moon. I doubt we even knew the word. I wonder if his pious mother ever knew. Yet Aldo had star power, and he could lead me to a more elevated and enchanted world.

SI introduced me to the Jesuits with whom I would spend twenty years after high school. It was a financial stretch for my parents to pay the tuition, but they believed that education was valuable. After my first year, Fr. Alexander Cody, a portly, venerable man with wispy white hair and somewhat effeminate manners, came to the rescue with a scholarship to keep me at SI. Cody was a born recruiter, a talent scout for the Society of Jesus ("the order"), who could spot a prospect a long way off. In 1948 he would shepherd four of us into the order in a big black sedan that crept down the pre-freeway Bayshore to the Los Gatos Novitiate. The other three entrants are still Jesuits. Jim Torrens, a life-long friend whom I met in frosh year, would spend many formative years with me. Our temperaments were quite different, and our spiritual paths verged away from one another. I think of him as a sterling sixteenth-century man who might be transported back to live with Ignatius in the Roman professed house alongside the *Gesù* church without a hitch. He would be trudging the muddy streets of Rome working with prostitutes and orphans. But Jim could never let himself think that Jesus might have been a non-divine, great spiritual Jewish master or that all theology is metaphor. This is baffling because Jim is a poet and where else would we meet so many metaphors. But I'm getting ahead of myself.

The boys high school was a positive experience for me. Young Jesuit teachers lifted me out of the narrow confines of my Oakland milieu, and introduced me to a wider world of learning. In the waning days of classical liberal arts education, we dabbled in enough Latin and Greek to give us a feel for the literature. Later we might dazzle people at cocktail parties with one-liners from Cicero, Virgil and Homer. We had some impressive lay teachers, but my teenage bonding was to a few "scholastics" (Jesuit seminarians). They exuded vitality, knowledge as well as a dedicated life. Nothing in Oakland could match them. They became models to emulate.

I didn't give much thought to their celibate status. Most of us had little contact with girls. I had no sisters, and the few dances and proms were largely perfunctory meetings. As a good student and editor of the school newspaper, I was ripe for picking as a future Jesuit. Their life style enticed me as a world of learning, camaraderie, and good works. The widespread respect for the priesthood among Catholics at mid-century gave clerical life a special aura of respectability. I decided to enter the order after high school, swept along by a wave of mixed motives. I could serve God, escape the frustrations of family life, and follow the enchanted Jesuit calling. This adventure attracted large novice classes of military veterans and wet-behind-the-ears high school grads in the years following World War II.

The road to the Los Gatos Novitiate led me farther away from *Nonno's* wine-making basement. In many ways, it had to be. I wasn't ready to recognize spirit in the world. I was immature and the Catholicism I knew enfolded me. I would have to soar like Icarus to gain a wider view. My religiously constructed wings would melt along the way. Yet this was the paradox of *Sol Invictus,* the unconquered sun, that draws us to climb and then drops us back to earth. Spiritual traditions point to this rhythm. Mystics like Buddha and Jesus experienced it.

1939: Natale, George, Katie, Gene

2

Grape-Picking Between Heaven and Earth

Our mind is capable of passing beyond the dividing line we have drawn
for it. Beyond the pairs of opposites of which the world consists,
other, new insights begin.

—HERMANN HESSE

THE LOS GATOS JESUIT Novitiate celebrated Vow Day on the feast of
the Assumption of the Virgin Mary into heaven on August 15. The
year was 1948 and the chapel was filled with expectant novices, their
fellows in humanistic study, and a large class of new entrants like me.
We hadn't had breakfast, because in those days Catholics fasted from
midnight before receiving communion. I don't know if it was the long
ceremony or some unarticulated doubt in my soul, but during the dramatic singing of the *Suscipe* ("Receive, O Lord, my whole being . . .") my
consciousness was suddenly "assumed" out of my body as I slumped
forward against the pew. I was able to leave the chapel and sit on its
metal-fringed steps. Was this spell an ominous sign at the start of my
Jesuit career? Perhaps a portent that I wasn't really fit for the demands
of the *Suscipe*?

These queries present themselves easily now as they could not have
then. My life experiences at eighteen were limited in comparison with
youths today. Mine was a world still steeped in a Depression mentality
of scarcity and leavened by the sacrifices of the World War. I was pre-
television, pre-easy-access to women, drugs, and rock and roll. I grew
up in an ethnic Catholic culture of unquestioned beliefs, although the
Jesuits expanded my horizons. My high school heroes, the scholastics,
had similar backgrounds. But, of course, I didn't realize this when I got
up from those linoleum stairs to eat breakfast with my new community.

There are at least two stories here. One tale describes my experiences in the late 1940s. But now I look back through a long telescope, only partially grasping my teenage sentiments. I'm telling a different story than that of my younger self. The tales are now entangled. The old man has the unfair advantage of misrepresenting himself as an adolescent. Since I can only experience my younger self from a distance, I inevitably skew the picture. Yet even an imperfect account of the past throws light on today's interpretations.

In the late forties, Jesuit formation took place in a semi-monastic environment. I use "monastic" here in the sense of intentional separation from secular life. It's ironic that an order that began as a movement away from monasticism should have ended up with many of its characteristics. Ignatius withdrew his followers from the life of vowed stability and choir duties to free them for active ministries in the new urban centers of the late Renaissance. But after the order's suppression by Pope Clement XIV in 1773, the newly reborn Jesuits of 1814 cultivated a defensive mentality toward the world and modern science. They became staunch defenders of a beleaguered papacy, and formed recruits in a mentality separate from the world. Italian Jesuits brought this re-monasticized vision for novices to California in the nineteenth century. It was life not only removed from the world, but also *contra naturam*. This struggle against nature supported the split in Catholic life between sacred and secular, church and world, sexuality and holiness.

Yet such thinking was satisfying for those immersed in it. It made me feel like a special person placed by God in a distinctive group lifted above the ordinary. Our immigrant Catholic communities supported this view. The laity looked on priests as a well-educated class that would bring honor to their humble origins. We were set aside by our black robes, Roman collars, and our isolation in the lovely hills of Los Gatos. We hinted at this dubious separateness during recreation periods. Looking down on Highway 17 on a weekend with its stream of traffic heading to the pleasures of Santa Cruz beaches, we would mutter: "of course, they're not really happy."

The novitiate was a constant round of disciplines from times of prayer and spiritual reading to mind-easing periods of work and some play. We usually took meals in a silent dining room listening to a reader. These readings often focused on an asceticism of physical and mental sufferings pleasing to God. God seemed to veer between expressions of love and the violent retribution of an abusive parent. Bells controlled everything, marking the start and finish of prescribed activities. Our godly boot camp was supposed to turn out loyal soldiers of Christ, papal commandos willing to travel to distant lands to spread the Kingdom. Such a militaristic vision of Jesuits was an ironic deviation from Iñigo of Loyola's idea of the *societas amoris*, a company of love. Soldierly disciplines influenced Ignatius, but his order was also supposed to imitate the peaceful ways of Christ. Yet from its earliest years, the Jesuits praised soldier-like ideals of going to foreign missions. Evangelism in the sixteenth century meant conquering false religions to save souls. It involved bringing outsiders into the Catholic fold. We looked on men chosen to go to the China missions, for example, if not as sacred kamikazes, at least as special souls who stood above the ordinary. I felt a certain awe when peers showed these qualities.

This concept of missionary zeal would change later in more pluralistic contexts. But during my early years as a Jesuit, its banners waved mightily. It was an "us against them" mindset whether we were dealing with godless Communists or the idolatries of the East. Of course, we would "go in their door," as the saying went, but only to come out our own, enticing them to Christ. The novitiate, a factory for manufacturing separations, reflected the Catholic Church for much of its history. I recall a gruesome example of this spirit when we gathered for a special blessing with the arm of Francis Xavier, an early companion of Ignatius. I can still see the fervent Irish-American priest who accompanied the arm making the sign of the cross over us with the ornate reliquary that housed it. This was the arm that baptized countless infidels into the true church of Christ.

Our Master of Novices, Francis "Dutch" Seeliger, was a convoluted character, neither frightening nor inspiring, who lived in some stratosphere removed from our young problems. I wonder what a sharp shrink would have made of him. But Seeliger, as the Italians would say, was not *cattivo*, mean or malicious. That minimalist statement actually counts for a lot in my view of humans. Though driven by demons and angels of his own, Dutch retained some common sense and a muffled note of humor as he chewed on his handkerchief during daily instructions in the *aula* (lecture room) or supervised the making of vow crucifixes in *taberna*, our workshop. My first vows crucifix still hangs prominently in my study among academic degrees. Dutch took a special glee in hand-working talent. Those who had this gift went up in his estimation. He also gave us the Spiritual Exercises, known as the thirty-day or Long Retreat. The Exercises aimed at fostering an environment for making important decisions. Its four "weeks" led the participant through fundamental themes like sin and death into meditations on the life of Christ. For its time, it was a remarkable combination of psychological and religious motives for self-reflection. Yet all I remember is how very long and somber it was as we labored through "points" (introductory lectures) and meditations on our knees virtually all day long. Only refectory reading and Dutch's voice broke the silence.

At one break for conversation during this retreat, a second year novice, Bob Jay, said that if I could only affect a limp, I would remind him of Ignatius at Manresa. Before his conversion from the military to church service, Loyola suffered a leg wound in the battle of Pamplona. During his recovery, he read medieval writings like Ludolph of Saxony's *Life of Christ* and devised the Spiritual Exercises. Jay's dubious compliment, however, disclosed a crucial theme that neither of us would have conceived at the time. If I weren't so pious and naïve, I should have affected a heavier limp and possibly even slouched to one side as I came and went. It would have been a clear sign that we were play-acting at the Exercises. Dutch would have kicked my behind for such mockery, maybe even before the assembly of novices. But in a less constrictive environment, my big limp might have sparked a lively dialogue on what the hell we thought we were doing.

Ignatius came to his Exercises as a mature individual who was responding to a real crisis in his life. He shaped the Exercises in the only idiom he knew, that of early sixteenth-century Spanish Catholicism. Both of these points go back to my limp. We youngsters were not coming to the Long Retreat out of any deep need based on our own life experiences. We were too young for this sort of thing. We were going through the paces, as it were, of someone else's spiritual experience. No wonder it was so tedious. It would not be hard to extrapolate from this example the perennial mistake of how the church chooses its leaders. Instead of finding leaders among lay people who have already had important spiritual experiences (like Ignatius), the institution insists on taking relatively immature men and running them through a make-believe world of seminary formation. Of course, the mandate of clerical celibacy virtually prescribes this manner of priestly selection. It was important to recruit them young before they would be lost to sexual attractions. At least, they should have encouraged us to take spiritual steps according to our real experiences. In recent decades newer ways of doing the Exercises in more individuated ways have improved on this collective retreat.

My limp would have brought up a second theme. Can a modern person really think and pray like an early sixteenth-century Spaniard? I doubt that we can appropriate such different experiences. We went through the forms of what seemed to be a serious conversion without embracing its substance. They gave us too much, too soon in too foreign a medium. In an odd way, our early mentors were defying a well-known principle of Thomas Aquinas: whatever is received is received according to the ability of the recipient. We could pretend to incorporate the inner life of Ignatius, but our immaturity as well as our cultural dissonance kept us from the outcome he had in mind.

Yet the disciplines of the novitiate were an introduction to a life of inner prayer. They also provided a broader knowledge of Jesuit and Catholic teachings. They opened up a new folder, as it were, in our mental computers, even if it was to remain largely empty until our real life experiences could summon up some files for it. If we were ever to come back to serious inwardness, it would be because the motives arose from genuine personal needs. At Los Gatos our piety was largely glued on from the outside, inducing us to follow the Jesuit "long black line."

The mutual influence of fellow Jesuits-to-be bonded us to the order. We children of the Depression were used to taking orders from parents and teachers. The forties were not a time of rebellion or permissiveness. Hard economic times made us curb our desires, and the war demanded submission to authority. Angelo Maffeo, a high school friend from Oakland, made a seemingly depreciating remark when he heard that I was about to enter the Jesuits. But he expressed the hard-headed practicalities that drove immigrant populations: "You'll get three squares a day in the order." He hinted that it was a move upward into the better-off life of Jesuits.

But the camaraderie of our advanced boys school eased us over the bumps of this odd life style. Despite the strictures against "particular friendships," we were able to develop personal bonds. Our instructors never discussed particular friendships as a defense against homosexual practices. They said little or nothing about sexual development in general. They preferred to fall back on Ignatius's famous dictum that concerning sex nothing need be said. He wanted us to imitate angelic conduct in this realm, whatever that might mean for young men with copious testosterone coursing through their un-angelic bodies. A better rationale for avoiding particular friendships was the argument to avoid cliques and get to know all novices during recreation and work periods.

I've noticed that outsiders ask about archaic disciplines practiced in early Jesuit training. These are the wearing of "chains" during meditation and Mass, as well as brief flagellation with knotted cords before going to bed during Lent. These quaint remnants of medieval monasticism were much more interesting in the telling than in actual practice. The chains consisted of small wire devices that fit around one's thigh, causing discomfort but no harm. The "whips" were small, light, string-like knotted cords that could sting, but leave no trace. We would kid about these practices later in our careers. There was always Brother X, wiser than the rest of us, who would whip his pillow when the bells sounded. Or Brother Y who conveniently wore his chains pointed away from his thigh. The novitiate had its pranksters who couldn't resist putting one over on a susceptible novice. These games probably contributed to sanity and friendship.

We never wore hair shirts in the Society, although we sometimes acted like hair shirts to one another. One such event is still memorable. A few of us conspired to persuade Brother C that the Master chose only special souls to wear a hair shirt. We then formed a rough hair shirt out of burlap and secretly inserted it into C's laundry bundle. There were red faces attempting to suppress laughter when Brother C revealed his burlap shirt while removing his cassock to wash dishes after dinner. It was a rather mean joke, but the real joy consisted in the mental campaign to gradually convince him to wear the sack as a sign of advanced holiness in the eyes of the Master. It was the elegance of briefly dropped hints in passing and hushed looks of awe at one so lucky to be among the elect.

In hindsight, the real lesson of chains, hair shirt, and whips was how gullible we were in that hot house environment. Actually, we were not too far removed from the brainwashing experiences of our contemporaries in the Korean War. Into this potpourri of ascetic oddities, I should cast the *Exercitium Caritatis*, the so-called Exercise of Charity, and one's subsequent prostration for forgiveness in the refectory, our large communal dining room. The *Exercitium* took place in a large room with one novice at a time kneeling before the Master. Other novices, seated in a circle, would rise to announce a defect or two of the kneeling Brother. This recitation of shortcomings was brief and usually not very penetrating. The Master guarded against the practice getting out of hand. No one got up and said that Brother Z was a flaming faggot. The purpose of the discipline was threefold: to instill a spirit of humility in the accused novice, to permit him to see and correct his deviant ways, and unfortunately, to encourage us to "rat" on one another to superiors.

For most Jesuits the *Exercitium* was just a passing hurdle in the march of the long black line, a practice quickly forgotten after the noviceship. But the attitude begun in this exercise could later foster distrust. It encouraged a mindset of reporting others to superiors, and for some it shut down easy communication with fellow Jesuits. There were times when it was responsible conduct to advise a superior of a serious problem. But it was also too easy to say things that were untrue, unimportant or unproven, thereby shattering trust.

But these odd practices were not as central to novitiate life as was the refectory. Most meals were taken in silence, except on occasions when the rector called out *"Deo Gratias"* as a signal to converse. The food was generally good. On a few special festivals, like August 15th (vow day), when, in the old Italian tradition of the California Province, many courses and four wines momentarily dispensed us from the vow of poverty and perhaps even the sin of gluttony. But the latter was of little consequence since Master Seeliger defined it as not being able to eat one more olive.

Of the three vows, poverty (chastity and obedience being the other two) was the most paradoxical. They explained it as a poverty of dependence. A Jesuit was not supposed to own his own property or to accumulate wealth. But the life-span security blanket of the order precluded the risk of real poverty. The vow of poverty came down to making one's life simpler. Today's peace and justice movement among Jesuits, with its attempt to serve the marginalized in society, accentuates the paradox of solidarity with the poor contrasted with the standard of living of some Jesuit communities.

The refectory linked nourishment of the body with food for reflection. It was a good experience to read to the community while an appointed priest at the main table called out corrections. The reader would then correctly repeat the muddled word. Frequently something funny appeared in the annals of the Society: "on this day in 1608, Father

Ludovici of the Italian Province died in the odor of sanctity." I always wondered about this odor. The reading that stands out in my time at Los Gatos was *The Seven Storey Mountain* by Thomas Merton. From my present vantage point, I'm struck by similarities in our life journeys. I was not born to Merton's privileged class, although I would later do doctoral studies at Columbia University whence Merton graduated shortly before entering the Trappists in Kentucky. Nor was I a convert to the church from a circle of incipient literati. Later, as a young priest and Columbia University graduate student, I celebrated a weekly Mass at Corpus Christi parish where Merton was received into the church.

What we had in common over the long haul was a movement away from narrow-gauge Catholicism to an appreciation for world religions and an attempt to incorporate their practices. *The Seven Storey Mountain*, Merton's first Catholic memoir, is replete with self-congratulation for leaving the secular world to embrace the higher rigors of the Cistercian order. Merton gradually developed a more conciliatory tone toward the world, as he struggled with issues of the Vietnam War and fell in love with a nurse during a hospital convalescence. The setting of his 1969 death in Bangkok at an inter-religious conference seemed very appropriate, since his later writings included many insights from Buddhism and Taoism.

In our early training we lived in a world of top-down Catholicism, symbolized by the magazine, *The Pope Speaks*. We bought into the idea that God spoke to us through our superiors in the Society, who in turn stood in a hierarchical line from rector to the pope. It seems amazing now that we would read this journal as though it represented God's will expressed by the Pontiff and relayed to us in Los Gatos hills by a series of intermediaries. There are, of course, clear organizational advantages to this line of command, as long as subordinates accepted its rationale. We were taught that by the vow of obedience we became pleasing to God. This environment induced considerable strain, especially among novices more susceptible to scruples. Many could not take the stress and left during early years of training. Such young men would disappear over night without a word said to the community. Superiors were probably afraid that those who left might inspire others to leave if their departure was made public. But our supervisors would have replied that the silent exits respected the privacy of those leaving.

The vow of obedience created inner stress in our rule-bound world. It could cause a splitting off from one's inner feelings. It fostered denying one's own mind in deference to a superior who stood in the place of God. Later we would learn about the importance of consulting with superiors and following one's own conscience (actually an old Catholic ethical teaching). Yet the overwhelming thrust of our training in obedience was at odds with any conscientious choosing from within. Even though the Ignatian Exercises were geared to help a person make important decisions, our inner choice-making was diminished by the constant demand to conform. It was another contradiction in an order that had drifted from early risk-taking to assembly-line production of recruits. The novitiate taught submission to authority every minute of the day.

Our mentors would have defended the system by saying that obedience was not merely an external rule. By submitting our wills to authority, they would argue, novices learned to internalize commands, making them their own. Moreover, they would insist that this first training in the Society called for bending the twig back to make it flourish later in the right direction. But our environment gave little or no encouragement to exercising one's own thought processes. Such personal reflection would have been seen as injurious to the spirit of the Jesuits. We were being prepared for an order in which we would often learn about a new appointment from the bulletin board. (In recent years, the order encourages consultation with superiors concerning one's choice of ministries.) But our training was a questionable endeavor of suppressing one's own mind and feelings.

Sports relieved some of the tension built up in the hot house milieu of formation. Basketball and baseball were favorite pass-times, in part because they lessened physical contact while providing good exercise. Maybe I should have wondered about my future success as a Jesuit when I struck out three times in one inning at the none-too-swift pitching of Jack Boyle who would go on to be a New Testament scholar. At nineteen I learned to swim at Los Gatos in a pool called Finnegan's Folly. Fr. Finnegan, a feisty, balding rector built the sandstone pool. The builders constructed the large building with the heaviest section on the downside of a sloping hill. The smallest earth tremor, especially in our California earthquake zone, would have challenged this strange engineering. But Finnegan had a personality to defy both gravity and divine providence.

Another novice, Jim Maher, an expert swimmer and diver, brought down on himself a reprimand for wearing a torn tee shirt. As his dives progressed, the shirt ripped this way and that, clinging to his well-defined body. Again, the ugly specter of sex rose in the guise of a suggestively torn tee shirt. Most of us were heterosexuals, but the all male surroundings gave me the novel experience of a special attraction to a few companions. Although not acted on, it was certainly a kind of sexual buzz. This phenomenon is well known to scholars of same-sex institutions like prisons, asylums and the military. But not knowing that at the time led to worries about my own orientation.

Only later did I realize why we didn't play touch football in our early years as Jesuits. Too much touch, even in such a hectic sport, threatened our chastity. The attitude toward games and other physical exercise was ambiguous. These activities promoted health and a measure of stress release. But our mentors also wanted to help us curtail nightly desires. Hard play or work would make us sleep sounder. Masturbation was a major no-no in the Catholic lexicon. It was one of those grave matters that could incur mortal sin and a teetering on the brink of hell. Contact sports also held the special danger of fostering homosexual conduct. We were a microcosm of the church's hang-ups about sex well before the child abuse scandals of recent times. A powerful dualism of mind and body held sway.

Another form of intense exercise, grape-picking, symbolized a competitive drive characteristic of the order. In the fall, all available hands gathered to pick grapes for the Novitiate Winery. We traveled in the back of open trucks to the hillsides of the Santa Clara Valley (now upscale housing developments). We harvested the vines hatless in the blazing sun (ignorant of skin damage). We greeted these all-day excursions as a welcome break from our lock-step life. I remember the fierce competition among those who raced to tally up the most boxes picked in a day. They would brag about being able to place their grape-juice encrusted jeans in the corner of a cubicle as a testament to their gung-ho spirit. This is how they would win souls for God. Their fervor to be perfect Jesuits, to please God, the unseen field *padrone*, drove them. Some of us sliced our way from vine to vine at a moderate pace, dragging the wooden boxes that could weigh forty pounds. I seemed to follow the biblical injunction to linger, each man under his vine. I had no desire to win the wine sweepstakes as I trudged across the plowed earth carrying a full box to stack at the end of the row. Some interior monitor (maybe my grandfather's "I'm religious but not fanatic") told me that enough was enough.

The hard work of grape-picking contributed to our support as it supplied free labor for the Novitiate Winery, a then thriving business for altar and dessert wines. But toil in the vineyards, strenuous sports and long walks in the hills were also disciplines to temper sexual impulses. Even our long black cassock entered into these calculations. It set us off (marking us as unavailable) from those engaged in normal sexual pursuits. It covered the body loosely from neck to ankle in a funereal hue symbolizing the death of our youthful sexuality. It was a sacrifice to a God who supposedly liked that kind of thing. We hid our maleness as a chador might conceal a Muslim woman's contours or a nun's habit cloak her body. The cassock also tended, especially in cultures where clerics did not wear long pants, to align them with womankind. Men in Latin countries frequently viewed priests as some kind of third sex.

In a world where homosexuals were not, almost by definition, supposed to exist, the cleric, deprived of symbolic male clothing, was in a sense neutered. The athletic jock mentality of some of my Jesuit colleagues can be seen as a vigorous attempt to counter this image. Our way of dressing, the cloister and restricted contact with outsiders made clerics appear unsexed. On a visit back to Los Gatos decades after leaving the order, I was struck by similar thoughts as I paused in front of the large, Lourdes-like replica of the shrine of Mary Immaculate. I recalled prayer devotions during May at this shrine. As we knelt saying the rosary, we were looking up at a life-sized statue of Mary with her heel resting on the head of a serpent, often a symbol of sex. She was crushing Satan. Her robe was very much like our cassocks, covering her body, making her acceptable and even venerable by neutering her. The whole notion of Mary Immaculate expressed the powerful drive to remove sex from any association with Jesus or his mother. I had no idea as a young devotee at Los Gatos about Marian devotions as driven by the celibate culture of clerics. They were projecting their own sexual resistance struggle on to the Virgin Mother. She became the sky goddess who rose above the allure of the flesh.

This organized withdrawal from sex made it all the more enticing. Master Seeliger, who spoke very rarely about the topic, did warn us in a roundabout way to beware the stormy attraction of "white caps." It was his code language for nurses who prowled hospital corridors preying on the purity of novices. I remember the special attraction of three young women whom I saw from my window. They were chatting near the winery. I felt a strong pang of loss, realizing that the vows would remove me from close contact with them for the rest of my life.

One Sunday I was strolling with my father and mother along the scenic path leading away from the shrine of Our Lady. Gino turned to me with his usual directness and asked: "Whatsamatta, you no like girls?" Katie countered with: "O, Gino, please. Don't bring that up." I probably gave him an idealistic answer. Yet his prescient query and the sadness at seeing the three girls were not enough to pull me away from the Jesuits. The camaraderie and adventure of the Society triumphed over my largely unawakened sexual leanings. It was an example of the inevitability of social influence. I was steeped in a Catholic culture that didn't let me grasp my narrow options.

Before our teaching years (called Regency), we took two years of humanities study (the Juniorate) and three years of philosophy. During these periods, I experienced a growing conflict between reason, as critical intellect, and the demands of loyalty to a church defensively stuck in the nineteenth century. We studied Greek and Roman classics in the original. But few of us made enough progress in those ancient languages to be able to read Sophocles and Virgil as literature. We struggled with grammar and vocabulary rather than absorb this literature in English. We failed to discuss it at a higher intellectual level.

I suspect that the best of our teachers would have relished thoughtful literary discussions. But they also knew that they were mainly equipping us with enough Latin and Greek for clerical studies. This symbolized a built-in paradox. The best kind of university learning stimulates innovation and many-sided criticism. Clerical education fostered acceptance of already defined truths. We were to think with the church, which meant defending positions taken by the hierarchy. This is, of course, an overstatement, especially for Jesuits, but the paradox was real. Many of us struggled against such limits through personal study and the inspiration of colleagues. As the years went on, our camaraderie expanded to lively intellectual exchanges among peers.

But the environment was not conducive to independent thinking. Life in the order called for loyalty rather than creativity, or perhaps some creativity at the service of loyalty. Our teachers, usually kind and intelligent men, were themselves products of the system. They were not about to rock the boat with ideas from the classics that might challenge Catholic and Jesuit thinking. I don't recall any serious, extended discussions in class about ideas raised by such literature or any pitched battles by contending students. Little or nothing touched my emotional mind. Themes have to grip us to remain in memory. They have to perplex and inspire us. This would later happen to me in graduate studies and in my life as a college professor and writer.

Even during our philosophical studies at Mount St. Michael's in Spokane, there tended to be a narrowing of our minds to fit the latest incarnation of Thomistic thought. (Thomas Aquinas in the thirteenth century wrote volumes of theology/philosophy that eventually became officially approved teaching.) We experienced more freedom at the Mount partly by mixing with the feistier men of the Oregon Province. I encountered a few teachers, like Cliff Kossel and Edmund Morton, who stimulated our minds. But even with such men, there were subtly imposed limits to investigation. We rarely read the great philosophers from Descartes through the Enlightenment. Hume and Kant, for example, were always posed as adversaries who questioned reason's ability to know absolute truth. Such thinkers were already listed in our textbooks as "*adversarii*" to be dismissed with pithy one-liners. Their fates were decided for us before we could take them seriously.

We studied updated versions of Thomism according to Etienne Gilson and Jacques Maritain with a friendly nod to Christian existentialists like Gabriel Marcel. Later Bernard Lonergan would join this approved list of philosophers. These were important thinkers. But they were corralled into safe channels to prepare us for theology in its pre-Vatican-II style. As candidates for the priesthood, we "proof-texted" philosophy to find arguments to sustain Catholic theology. Many of us came to realize this intellectual determinism when we read more widely on our own or during later graduate studies. Although this Jesuit education was a far cry from the mind-constricting literalism of a Bible school, it suffered from its own form of authority-driven fundamentalism. The official church lined out our mental playing field. We could go only so far without upsetting the dogmatic applecart.

But these thoughts did not bother me much during early years of Jesuit training. I was pleased to receive an education that was far more advanced than anything I had known before. Moreover, the isolated environment of the Mount held at bay other worldly enticements. Friendships with other Jesuits expanded to enjoy sports, movies, music, and lots of laughs. A couple of companions kept us in stitches by impersonating the idiosyncrasies of superiors and teachers. It was our way of leveling authorities in an authoritarian system. We settled into like-minded groups as the emphasis on avoiding particular friendships faded. I was introduced to classical music and Gregorian chant, an appreciation that has lasted a life time. It is interesting to realize how naïve we were about homosexuals in the community. Gay bonding and acting out of the seventies was a long way off. One gay companion called me "gorgeous," and another sought my company. I sensed what was going on, but it didn't seem worth labeling at the time.

I was also being led into the political world as I cast my first ballot for Adlai Stevenson in 1952. My left-leaning politics were shaped in those early years. Jesuit Louis Toomey's "Blueprint for the South" acted as a catalyst for opening my mind to the social teaching of the church and its bearing on issues like a living wage and distributive justice. The Society in America had also established centers for social justice at a few Jesuit universities. Jesuit labor priests actually organized workers in collaboration with unions. Moreover, most of my companions were children of immigrant, ethnic Catholics. Their cultural backgrounds were steeped in working class adherence to labor unions and the Democratic Party.

1955 was a milestone year for my writing career as I placed my first article in *America*, the national Jesuit cultural and spiritual magazine. I had written a few pieces for local church publications, but nothing of wide circulation. That first *America* article, largely a report of a philosophy conference, oddly enough characterized much of my subsequent writing. I was impressed by attempts to dialogue across previously uncrossed borders. I was drawn to what I would later call the pluralistic mind in religion. This simple article showed a desire to probe beyond given confines. It also seems to be consistent with the general theme of this memoir: how to move beyond our provincialisms to speak a cosmopolitan language of spirit.

If that article echoed my intellectual bent, my lead role in Shakespeare's *Coriolanus* became a prologue to what a future Provincial termed my headstrong willfulness. John F. X. Connolly, a handsome and basically kind superior, warned me of such a character flaw just before my final vows as a Jesuit. He was passing on to me the assessments of other Jesuits "who knew me well." When I now look at his letter, I realize how different Connolly and I were. He was a good Jesuit of the old school, a rule-bound person lacking critical assessment about changes needed in the church. The letter cites "a certain immaturity, a tendency to naïve judgments concerning distant or recent achievements in the church and the Society . . . joined to a strong determination . . . wedded to change . . . and a tactlessness in expressing your views . . ." By the sixties, I had written articles about harmful traditions in the church and the order. I had spoken publicly about changes I saw useful for reform. That letter was written in 1965 just before watershed developments in clerical life. In a way, we were both right. The Provincial was judging from within the box and I was looking over its edge at new horizons. But I'm getting ahead of my tale. I open a photo album and look at myself as *Coriolanus* in flowing Roman toga. I am no longer that young man with dark hair and chiseled features, pacing in the boiler room underneath the swimming pool belting out the bard's lines in fervent preparation for the play.

Yet I see myself as a kind of *Coriolanus* in the context of church authority. I would associate only with his leadership qualities, especially his willingness to take a stand, not his dictatorial penchant. I've wondered if this attitude arose in part as a reaction to my father's domineering. Or maybe it came from *Nonna*, who had an independent mind. But the Jesuits are partially responsible for my *Coriolanus* stances. The order was trying to pull off an impossible educational task. They emphasized loyalty to the church, but the same mentors could not hide Jesuit history that got the order thrown out of thirty-five countries and suppressed by a pope. It is not for nothing that their detractors invented the term, "jesuitical." The Jesuits, whatever their faults, have never been viewed as pious conformists. Perhaps the impossible goal of training obedient Voltaires is a key element of the Society's genius. They taught me to struggle with such polarity and to live the consequences.

Yet whatever seeds of rebellion were germinating in those first seven years in the order, I was still a "practicing Catholic." At twenty-five I was emotionally retarded in terms of close relationships, especially with women. The order kept us safely isolated from the ups and downs of sexual relations. This was one of many unresolved issues. Major Christian doctrines were infallible statements calling for unflagging belief. A deeper faith was confused with this belief system. I had no understanding of theology as metaphor. I had little sense of the impact of history on religious development. Nor had I applied Darwin via Teilhard de Chardin to the evolutionary march of religions. Despite all our Jesuit retreats, I didn't understand that contemplatives showed the best way of resolving faith and reason. Training in obedience kept me cut off from the urgings of both conscience and gonads. I was a young man full of good will. But I was living in animated suspension between an ill-conceived heaven and a largely unknown earth.

1948: SACRED HEART NOVITIATE

3

New Enthusiasm and Lingering Doubts

God picks up the reed-flute world and blows.
Remember the lips where the wind-breath originated,
and let your note be clear . . . Be your note.

—RUMI

ASSIGNED TO TEACH FOR three years at St. Ignatius High School in San Francisco in 1955, I hardly realized the impact of clerical culture on my life. I was too close to it, like a fish swimming in an unexamined pond. The new experience was exciting. For the first time in seven years I was leaving the monastic isolation of hilltops in Los Gatos and Spokane for the hurly burly of San Francisco. I would be teaching English and social studies to teenage boys only a few years my juniors at the school from which I entered the Jesuits. I would also be close to family across the bay. We were thrown into teaching without much preparation. It was sink or swim as best we could. Other scholastics had done it and survived. But in many ways we were not up to the changes in American Catholic culture of the fifties.

The turbulent sixties make us think of the Eisenhower era as a world of normalcy where ex-GIs sired large families and traditional church attendance increased. But under the cloak of business as usual, some were already questioning authority. The Korean War with its loss of life and unclear outcome dulled the full-throated patriotism of World War II. The McCarthy hearings made many less willing to accept inquisitional techniques imposed by authorities. Yet Joe McCarthy's demonizing of Communism was not far removed from Catholic anti-communist hysteria. Anti-Communism gave the church a clear enemy against which to define itself. Catholics didn't think about church reform when the red threat was at the gates. Even the Virgin Mary whispered secretly about Communism at Fatima.

Yet lock-step anti-Communism was beginning to fade. The GI Bill allowed young Catholics in great numbers to go to college, a breeding ground for independent thinking. Such people made up their own minds about using contraceptives. They questioned the Catholic ways of their less educated elders. I got to know John Tracy Ellis in San Francisco just after he published a landmark critique of Catholic higher education in 1955. He decried the lack of serious research in Catholic schools. Intellectual journals like *Commonweal* excoriated McCarthy's techniques. And lay ventures like the Christian Family Movement were developing a self-directed laity. The seeds of Catholic feminism sprouted with women like Patty Crowley in CFM. Four decades later I interviewed her on elder wisdom and her work in prison ministry for women.

Then there was Elvis whose voice and swaying hips challenged older sexual mores. Catholic ecumenists had already been observers at major Protestant conferences. And Cardinal Angelo Roncalli, soon to be Pope John XXIII, had experienced the sclerosis of fortress Catholicism from his years in Turkey and France. When he threw open the windows of *aggiornamento* in 1959, he unleashed an insurgency against the mindset of Pius X who condemned modernist Catholic thinkers for embracing new knowledge about Bible and dogma. Already in the fifties, some were envisioning changes in the church, and the New Theology was rising in France.

I saw only snatches of this cultural change as I trudged up and down the hills around St. Ignatius High, adjacent to the University of San Francisco campus, during long days of teaching and extra-curricular activities. We started at five a.m. and ended late with a glass of wine in the common room of the "barracks." Military barracks on the USF playing fields were leftovers from officer training days of World War II. These lodgings at the bottom of campus signified a generational struggle between scholastics and the "Old Sweets" who lived in Welsh Hall at the top of the hill. C. M. Buckley, a fellow scholastic, coined the ironic "Old Sweets" phrase to denote Jesuit priests who lived by semi-monastic rules and insisted that we do the same. In our lowly barracks, we were the groundlings grumbling about annoying rules, like participating in Litanies after dinner. (This was a communal recitation of the Litany of the Saints and other oral prayers.) We were sleep-deprived teachers with class preparation, student papers, and football practice to deal with the next day. Yet the Old Sweets controlled the high ground of expectations that would determine whether we were fit to go on to theology and the priesthood. A number of scholastics received an extra year or two of Regency for their escapades challenging the world of clerical obedience. Either by temperament or by what I learned as a child avoiding Gino, I managed to outwit the controllers, working under the conviction that it was better to ask forgiveness than permission.

Our hectic schedules as high school teachers usually kept our minds off bigger personal questions about long-term choices. Such issues loomed temporarily in the summer when some companions left the order. Jesuit officials referred to these leave-takings as "defections," a word that implied negativity rather than a positive choice for a different life. Since Catholic theory at that time defined the professional religious life as the highest state attainable, departures inevitably meant that some defects were at work in those who left. These deficiencies were usually attributed to lack of personal relations with God. Those who left ceased being men of prayer, it was said. From such weakness, a spiritual domino pattern of collapse ensued. The defectors would stop being obedient and they would fall into the sensual styles of the secular world. Rarely did we hear that perhaps religious life itself was poorly adapted to the needs of the times. That degree of open criticism was unlikely in the late fifties when the structures of American Catholicism seemed very solid and young men in large numbers continued to enter religious orders.

The rumblings of the earthquake to hit the clergy in another decade were muted. I was energized by contact with students in class and in my role as moderator of the debate team. We scholastics often became role models for some of the better students, just as our Jesuit teachers had been for us. These close contacts with boys were gratifying and sustaining. I am still in touch with students from that time. And our own scholastic comrades were plentiful enough in those days to instill a mutual camaraderie that in some cases has lasted a life time. Half a century later I regularly contact former Jesuits on an internet list called "Companions." Little did I realize, however, that the earthquake of 1955 in the Bay Area would symbolize the tectonic shift in the church a few years hence.

Near noon I was leaning against the window sill of my 4D classroom. This was my first year of teaching, so I had my hands full trying to get a few ideas across while maintaining discipline. Unlike my academically successful 4A class at the start of the morning, the 4D-ers saw school as prison time. They wanted to bolt from the wardens at noon and have a smoke. Then it happened. The room and the chandeliers began swaying, and I felt myself pitched back against the open windows. Student faces turned ashen as their customary swagger ebbed away. Minutes later Fr. Dave Walsh, the Prefect of Discipline, came on the loudspeaker: "Everyone is to stay in his classroom. There shall be no more earthquakes." Later I thought how consistently his command characterized the obedience system of the Society and the church. Orders from the top, from those who represented God, would save us.

Yet the fears of some were not stilled. In the classroom next door, rotund Fr. Leo Marine leaped under his desk, covered his head and shouted to the class: "Repeat after me the Act of Contrition: 'O my God, I am heartily sorry for all my sins . . .'" Humor at every turn saved our sanity. Fr. Marine was a standup comic without knowing it, a Chaplin who didn't know he was Chaplin. Classmate Bob Maloney and I almost destroyed the Easter vigil at the St. Elizabeth Home for Unwed Mothers near USF when we got into terrible suppressed laughing fits while serving his Mass.

Now I see how much the American Catholic culture of the late 1950s sustained my choice of a Jesuit career. On a personal level, bolstered by my own youthful energy, I enjoyed the demanding regimen, the special friendships with students, and companionship with other scholastics. I was also drawn on by prospects of a lifetime of writing and involvement in the order's universities. The priesthood, too, seemed to be a noble profession, despite the shipwrecked older Jesuits I saw at USF. They seemed sad, lonely, and resentful old men, sometimes given to alcoholism.

Yet for me the mid-century church bolstered personal optimism. Catholics still held the church in high regard despite its narrow-mindedness and dead traditions. The supporting Catholic culture was a kind of communion of saints, however tarnished their halos. The generation of our parents and grandparents still placed the clergy on pedestals. They might have known about problems of sex and liquor, but a spirit of loyalty kept both clergy and laity quiet. A culture that suppressed scandal overcame public exposure of problems. Compare the seeming solidity of priesthood in the fifties to today's milieu of sex abuse and deep turmoil. Moreover, the large cohorts of those entering the order after World War

II further supported our sense of self-esteem and new potential. Such large classes made us feel part of a new adventure.

But the spiritual training we received in those days was inadequate for moving toward the Jesuit ideal of becoming a contemplative in action. Retreat givers would talk about developing a personal relationship with Christ, but only a gossamer thread of rules and rites upheld us. Few had developed serious contemplative ways. Half asleep, we scrambled up the hill at dawn each morning to serve Mass for an equally sleepy priest who mumbled quickly though the Latin ritual in a side chapel of St. Ignatius Church. It was still the era of the private Mass, daily communion, and a theology of *ex opere operato* (as long as the priest generally intended to do what the church mandated at Mass, the sacrament worked.). And the old nostrum of "Keep the rules and the rules will keep you" led to the cat and mouse games of getting around superiors.

In quiet moments on the orange Key System trains that took me across the bridge to Oakland for a family visit, I was bothered by somber questions about the path I had chosen. Was the semi-monastic struggle worth the stress? Why did such a life please God more than living in the world? If God privileged such a lifestyle, what did that say about the image of such a divinity? Why would the great deity of the universe care about celibacy or masturbation? I didn't yet have the intellectual tools to grapple well with such queries, but they were simmering below the surface. What was I going to do about my own sexuality? I felt a kind of sadness as the train rumbled along carrying me on pre-determined tracks high up on the Bay Bridge. More than any intellectualizing about the *contra naturam* aspect of my life, a mood of sadness weighed me down. Now we saw more women than in earlier isolated settings, but there was little direct contact. High school girls, too young for serious interest, were only fleeting appearances at football games and debates. After a good home-cooked meal and a visit with Cooka, my heavier sentiments about sex would pass. He would greet me with his right fist hitting into his left palm: "John Mangini, report to me for confession," adding a brisk salute. Who wouldn't laugh at his self-referential riff on his time in the army. Moreover, lack of marital bliss at home would put a damper on my dreams of romance. But the sad feelings just went below deck waiting to rise again.

I was excited to be assigned to study theology in Louvain, Belgium in 1958. The four-year course was preparatory to ordination. To live in a French-speaking house and have a chance to travel in Europe came as a surprise and challenge. Fellow scholastics, Jim Torrens, Ed Malatesta and I set out in June by train for Quebec City to study French. It was then that I started to keep a journal. Now these journals of half a century are stacked around my computer, a mute testament on myself. I've hardly read them since I wrote them. So, it's like opening a book on someone else, even though I recognize the person. An Ignatian theme comforted me in that transition. I hoped to work in the Society for the good of souls. Somehow the various sacrifices seemed worthwhile in that light.

But I wonder now about working for the good of souls. As the train came into Grand Central Station, I wrote those lines about saving souls with commitment. I still agree with the value of helping others in useful ways, but I am much less interested in saving their souls for heaven. I leave that to God, if she has a heaven in store for us. Nor am I interested in working for souls apart from their bodies. In fairness to Ignatius, he, too, wanted to help the illiterate, the prostitutes and even the fat Cardinals in ways that would benefit a unity of body and soul. But I am less sanguine than he about the whole enterprise of saving souls, of converting others, of bestowing on them true doctrine. That impulse presupposes that we know the truth and are called to impart it to the unsaved. This stance leads to much mischief in the world over against a dialogical approach that speaks one's convictions without presuming to know the mind of God. Moreover, I am much more persuaded now by Taoist insights on letting things be and "not-knowing."

The summer in French Canada was a plus as I tried to keep my new French language learning separate from the Italian I picked up as a child. My observations of religion veered from odd feelings about the grandi-ose rituals with claims of miracles at the shrine of St. Anne de Beaupré to surprise about reports that more than half of Jesuit scholastics in Montreal were under psychiatric care. There were at least two religions, I concluded, in Catholicism and they differed intensely. One was the popular religion of ritual and devotions, while the other existed on the frontier between psychological balance and the demands of the vows in modern culture. In my journal, I wrote about putting aside accidents of Catholicism to center on the basics adapted to the modern world. St. Anne de Beaupré fell among the accidents. I was still a rationalist.

Now I realize that people practice devotions of religion as basic to their beliefs. Symbolic ritual performances from Mecca to Benares to St.

Peter's Square characterize religion. These forms of *bhakti*, devotional yoga, underscore what early Christians described as the apophatic dimension, meaning that the mind alone could not fully understand the divine. Rational theology, that wonderful metaphorical play of theologians, is itself a kind of koan for the seeker. The singing congregants at St. Anne's or in my grandmother's Italian mission churches were expressing what Karl Marx, that secularized Jewish theologian, called a deep longing for consolation and transcendence in a suffering world. His critique of religion as "opium of the people" didn't deny the genuine longing, but criticized its abuse. Yet in Quebec that summer, I was convinced that the new Catholicism of progressive theology, change in the church and modern psycho-spirituality would reform religious life. I hadn't read Meister Eckhart, and his experiencing the "ground source" of the God beyond God . . . in the stillness far removed from our speeding concepts. And I hadn't spent enough time on my meditation pillows.

I haven't lost interest in institutional reform because humans will always institutionalize for better or worse. Catholic teaching on sexuality, invented mainly by celibate male clerics, is particularly in need of reform. The journey to Europe underlined these pelvic tensions in the church. I could guess that those scholastics seeing shrinks in Montreal were struggling with straight or gay sexual issues. On a long bicycle trip on a scenic island near Quebec, Ed Malatesta and I stopped to rest on benches that we soon realized were in a lovers' lane. An attractive couple across the road was fully involved. Ed kept telling me that as young Jesuits in mufti we should move along. I said that we had to be in the world as it was, not running from it. As the amorous exchanges became more intense, he got up and started to move away. I sat there a while longer to make my point.

On the Saturnia, one of Mussolini's early transatlantic vessels, I developed a habit of lounging on a deck chair after a swim. The ship's chaplain, a pompous Italian Monsignor, who treated table waiters superciliously, berated me for public nudity. If I continued like this, he said, I would become a scandal to the faithful and endanger my priesthood. I thought I was pretty modest in boxer type swim trunks. I so disliked this conceited oaf that I made a point of occupying the deck chair every day as a clerical nude. It was on the Saturnia that I encountered my first male assignation attempt in a public rest room. The request came quickly as we stood at urinals. I brushed him off, but the incident played on my mind. I had very little insight into the homoerotic world, but it made me wonder about the deck chair. When the ship docked in Lisbon, Jim, Ed and I took a long walk at night along the bustling Avenue of Liberty. A young guy stopped us with "I can get you beautiful women cheap." We were not ready for Lisbon's sex workers, but I wondered out loud if they wore the white caps of Dutch Seeliger's fantasy nurses in Los Gatos.

Seeing Pompeii on a sweltering day made me think of so many churches that had turned into museums if not ruins. My first impressions of the church in Europe bespoke backwardness, a sense of not keeping up with modern civilization. The clergy's cassocks and their separate lives needed updating. A trip to Castel Gandolfo seemed to confirm these impressions as Pope Pius XII came out to bless us in his last year. The aged pontiff exemplified the last remnants of royalty in an age moving toward democratic ways. Yet the same day I visited with seminarians from the American College who vacationed near Castel Gandolfo. They hailed from one of the earliest democracies in the West, but they hankered after aristocratic *Romanità* and its career advantages. Arriving back in Rome at what I thought was a reasonable hour, I found the Jesuit house bolted. By making enough noise, I roused a Brother who let me in. It was just one more example of living behind the raised drawbridge. In a meeting with Father General Janssens, I noticed his pained surprise when he heard we were on our way to Belgium via Rome. I continued to smile, remembering that Jesuits were supposed to travel to distant parts of the world maybe even by circuitous routes.

My first visit to relatives near Lucca and Genova remains important. I have been back a number of times with a growing continuity of family and place. They were country people, *contadini*, on both sides of large families. It was easy to notice physical similarities and mannerisms. The *Lucchesi* spoke the king's Italian, but the *Genovesi* slipped into the dialect I heard around my grandmother's home in Oakland. I remembered her stories about the homestead above Chiavari at *Pian dei Ratti* and the stream that ran behind the house with the family cow grazing on its banks. Then I saw the view of the church of Soglio across the valley from the rustic bedroom where *Nonna* was born. I slept in the very bed where she came into this world. We went to Mass in a small stone chapel near family property, and we ate pasta *a la Genovese* and sautéed vegetables that I knew from my own kitchen. The fruity wine was homemade.

At the time, I would not have thought of these experiences as religious. After all, I was on my way to Louvain for serious theology. I was studying for the priesthood, which had to do with Scriptures and sacraments. That was the true religion, the path to salvation, wasn't it? I failed to relate spirit to these rolling hills and to my cousins in their individual ways. Angela, who never married, talked about the German prisoners of war who camped nearby. She took me by bus to the shrine of the *Madonna di Mont'Allegro* where crutches hanging on walls reminded me of cures claimed at St. Anne de Beaupré. Cousin Maria introduced me to her cow and showed me how she used a scythe to cut hay. Of course, we took the obligatory walk up the steep hill of Soglio to visit the *camposanto* where our forebears were buried. That Italian word for cemetery underscores the sacredness of the burial field itself. *Pian dei Ratti* was giving me a lesson only understood later about connection to family and earth. Study of theology would withdraw me from such primordial experiences that energized humanity from our hunter-gatherer days.

Louvain turned out to be a mixture of opportunity and dogged persistence. The skies were gray, the food poor, and the building at Eegenhoven a fortress of discomfort. Some of the rules, like going to Litanies, were aggravating. The latter became especially irritating when Father Minister took it upon himself to knock on doors to discover laggards at community prayer times. Yet even he wasn't a serious cop. Rather he resembled the parked police car reminding speeders to check their consciences. On the whole, European clerics were less legalistic than their American counterparts. They didn't really believe that if we kept the rules, the rules would keep us.

New opportunity happened one day when I was bouncing along the cobblestones on a community bicycle in downtown Louvain. A small group had gathered around an electronics shop window. There on black and white television I saw the rotund new pope with the large head and bigger smile blessing us from his balcony in Rome. Little did I realize in the fall of 1958 how much Angelo Roncalli would change my life. This old man would soon open the Pandora's box of Vatican II.

Some of our teachers at Louvain were ready for John XXIII. It was as if he said to them: "Go for it, guys." One of these, Georges Dejaifve, became my mentor. He spoke English well, and had been involved in ecumenical conferences. Moreover, he had the soul of a democrat. He knew that Catholic structures couldn't remain in the defensive posture of the "one true church." Georges liked Americans despite our naïveté. We represented a democratic spirit less obvious in European clerics and we had good times together. He fully enjoyed listening to the Nixon-Kennedy debates with us in 1960 as we shared Stella Artois beer late into the night. Jean Galot, fresh from studies in Rome, was his opposite. His Christology relied on the authority of papal and conciliar statements rather than the Scriptures. The furthest thing from his mind was a Jewish Jesus who wouldn't have recognized himself had he read Galot's class notes. His fierce energy and heavy five-o'clock shadow reminded me of Rasputin. He presented Mary as a quasi divinity. These positions, however, got him promoted to the Rome of Cardinal Ratzinger and Opus Dei, where in recent times he became a hammer of "heretics."

We were lucky to be close to the University of Louvain. When I didn't have to study for exams at Eegenhoven, I took courses in sociology of religion at the university and I read widely on topics not covered in theology classes. My venture into social science put me in touch with Jan Kerkofs, a Flemish Jesuit sociologist who has done important work on the state of the European Catholic Church and its vanishing clergy. After a very long hiatus, I recently had occasion to communicate with him concerning my book (*Passionate Uncertainty: Inside the American Jesuits*, co-authored with Peter McDonough, University of California, 2002). Kerkofs showed me the value of scientific study of religion. Another important influence at the time was reading Milton Yinger, the American sociologist of religion. He helped me understand Christianity as the result of many social forces. Joining these insights with readings in church history made it clearer that our religious beliefs derived from the ever-changing imaginations of theologians.

Belgian Jesuit Edouard Boné, professor of anthropology at Louvain, opened up our evolutionary heritage. In previous seminary studies, no one talked intelligently about the evolution of the earth and humanity. Father William Gaffney at the Mount was a natural stand-up comedian, but he was also very anti-Darwinian. Later I thought about his infusion of souls into monkeys as a kind of mockery of God. It struck me as such an inelegant procedure for the Master Mechanic. I thought of God saying: "Damn it, Gabriel, I forgot to infuse souls into the proto-stuff at the Big Bang. Get down there and infuse souls into those hominids." We were a very long way from the theology of Thomas Berry who talks about revelation in the context of a universe story, rather than in the limited scope of the Bible. I started reading Teilhard de Chardin, the French Jesuit paleontologist, whose work set the human journey of evolution in a much wider context. As I bounced along the cobblestones of Louvain on a bicycle, my backside announced a very personal sense of my relation to the earth. I had a hunch that this was part of Teilhard's education, too.

Our American community at Eegenhoven numbered about twelve to fifteen at any one time. It was a chosen exile that taught us much about tolerance, adaptation, and an international attitude. We developed reasonable facility in French. But the stress of foreign-language speaking and the weight of dealing with somber Belgian customs made huddling with fellow citizens even more pleasurable. It was customary on Thanksgiving to gather for an American party in downtown Louvain. Occasionally other Jesuits roaming the continent would join us. So it was that Bill Richardson, who would become a noted Heidegger scholar and psychotherapist, came bearing a gift of *Kirschwasser* from Innsbruck. It went down so smoothly that no one realized that the traveler had delivered us a liquid *coup de grâce* at the end of a meal with plenty of wine.

We stumbled back late to Eegenhoven, traipsing in twos and threes through the darkened streets. The next morning a black cincture (the belt-like tie around our cassocks) had been pinned to the bulletin board. René Carpentier, our moral theology teacher, had been up very early to celebrate Mass at a convent. He had picked up the cincture that one of us dropped in front of a bordello. We quietly blamed this perversion on Walt Gordon, a Falstaff-like Californian, whose spirit of merriment made him unconscious of practical things like securing his cincture. Soccer wasn't our game, but we enjoyed watching skilled Belgians and Spaniards go at it. We formed a basketball team that consistently lost to our younger expats at the American College (seminary) in town.

We spent part of our summer vacation at a vacated *lycée* or high school in Namur. It wasn't very relaxing to go from one stone fortress to another, so some of us went AWOL for a few days, trusting our thumbs and the kindness of strangers. For all my dislike of dressing like a woman, the cassock was a sure way to get a ride in rural areas. Dick McCafferty and I took no provisions or extra clothing, since we thought we could get back in one day. But the villages and landmarks around Sedan seduced us so that we hung out like wandering mendicants. A parish priest graciously took us in and deposited us the next morning at a likely crossroad for hitch hiking. Our visit to the ossuary at Verdun, which houses the bones of soldiers who died in the First World War, made a strong impression. A year later I had similar experiences on a trip to "The Valley of the Fallen" near Madrid, a shrine containing the remains of the deceased in the Spanish Civil War. With the optimism of a liberal, I thought society could move beyond the Hobbesian war of all against all. Yet the ossuaries and the killing fields of Cambodia, Bosnia, Rwanda and Darfur remind us of our vicious heredity. When we walked back into the community at Namur, nobody had missed us. That was both good and not so good. Our superiors were not about to take roll with grown men. But I also wondered how long it would take for them to find me if I dropped dead in my room.

The thought of dying alone was symbolic of the crisis I experienced just before ordination. A counselor, *Père* Hostie, summed it up as a problem of faith and family. The first part was largely intellectual, the second affective. Did I really want to be ordained? The struggle was showing up in neck pain that took me to a doctor. Stress was the diagnosis. The faith dimension of this anxiety was not about whether I believed in God, but whether I trusted the teachings of the church enough to become its official representative. The theology underlying dogmas such as the divinity of Christ or the infallibility of the pope seemed unconvincing. We were not taught to see theological doctrines as metaphorical. In ethics I respected the church's social justice tenets, but I didn't agree with its positions on birth control, divorce, and other sexual teachings. It was 1961, just before Vatican II where the issues mentioned above would not be resolved, but a new openness would flourish. My spiritual director *Père* LeCocq reminded me of Charles de Foucauld's dictum: wanting to believe was enough in the eyes of God. Le Cocq didn't see any impediments to my being ordained. For him it was just jitters before taking the plunge. *Père* Hostie, however, didn't try to tip the balance. He left it up to me.

The other part of my *crise* focused on *foyer*: family and sex. As a Jesuit, I had already vowed myself to chastity, which precluded marriage. But the priesthood intensified what I was relinquishing. Psychology and church history invited me to question celibacy. If the church re-established a married clergy, would I remain a Jesuit? As much as I admired the order, my answer would have been no. How much was I just carried along against my true feelings by joining the Society as a teenager? Now I found myself trying to decide a life course, one of whose central tenets, celibacy, was under question. No wonder my neck stiffened. I even complained to doctors about aching testicles. How very appropriate. My body was trying to tell me something. But I fell back on the idealism that carried me this far. In a long letter to my mother, written a few days before ordination, I spoke in glowing, almost unctuous theological statements about this new step. No doubt, I believed those overblown concepts at the time, but much of it was also wishful thinking. It probably took that kind of exaggerated self-convincing to counter my doubts.

I was ordained a priest in Brussels on August 5, 1961. To this day I exchange messages in early August with Jim Torrens, SJ, who was in our ordination group. As I look again at the photos of the ceremony, I wonder about how such commitments stay with us and also change. I have long stopped seeing myself as a cultic priest, one who leads sacred ceremonies. I'm not opposed to such roles for ministers. As religious communities grow, they naturally develop a leadership group for preaching and sacrament. Yet Jesus was not a cultic priest but rather a teacher and healer. After ordination I traveled to northern Spain, staying at a Jesuit seminary near Bilbao. On the way back to Louvain, I visited Avila and Lourdes. Near the old walls of Avila, I recall a fair with many goats brought in from the surrounding countryside. I wasn't aware then of how important the contemplative or mystical life would mean to me later. But I did think of St. Teresa's comment that she would rather have a wise counselor than a pious one.

At the shrine in Lourdes I met Ed Malatesta and his parents. I've always been turned off by the commercialism around such places, but that may be an excess of elitism in myself. People have to make a living. The faith of the pilgrims was impressive. On returning to Eegenhoven, I was feeling sick. The infirmary Brother looked at my eyes near a window and pronounced that I had hepatitis. Fellow Americans, Jim Torrens and Tom O'Malley brought me meals only to get the infection themselves. No good deed goes unpunished. Our rector *Père* Louwers offered to send me to Nice for a rest, but I insisted on going to London. In his excitable way, he finally said: "*Mon Père*, I wash my hands of it." After my first white-knuckle jet plane flight, I stayed with the Jesuit community in Old Windsor. When I felt strong enough, I moved to the famous and musty Farm Street house in London's Mayfair district. I had to persuade Walt Gordon, then a student at the University of London, to go see "Young Man Luther" with Albert Finney. Walt was worried about local rules discouraging clerics from going to the theatre. I won out by convincing him that we could go in shirt and tie.

At the end of four years of theology, our final oral exam before four professors, was called the *Ad Gradum*. This test would determine our status or "grade" in the order. If we did well in the exam, we could become "professed" Fathers with a special vow of obedience to the pope. We would also become more eligible for special studies, that is, going on to pursue a doctorate in a subject helpful to Jesuit schools. Moreover, as professed Fathers, we could occupy higher offices in the Society like rector or provincial superior. The next grade down for those who didn't do so well in the *Ad Gradum* was spiritual coadjutor. These priests would serve in high schools and parishes or as hospital chaplains and similar activities.

My problem with the *Ad Gradum* was the conflict between indoctrination and freedom of expression. If one had a photographic memory and a reasonable control of Latin, he could ace this exam, perhaps with highest honors. Such a person would most likely not be a creative thinker, but a spectacular memorizer. There was always some room to argue for less popular positions in the exam, but these had to be carefully placed in the orbit of church doctrine. Before ordination candidates for the priesthood took the Oath Against Modernism. Taken in the solemnity of the chapel, this oath was set in the context of Pius X's condemnation of Catholic liberals at the turn of the twentieth century. The Modernist oath embraced conformity to Rome and discouraged creative thinking. We looked on it as one of those things we had to do to get our priestly credentials. Few people, including most of our professors, took it seriously. It was like getting your passport stamped.

My departure from Louvain became a Cinderella event. After pushing the last set of dirty dishes through the dishwasher, I changed into clerical suit and Roman collar, boarded a plane, and flew to Rome, where a black limousine with capped chauffeur whisked me toward the Vatican. Well, almost. As we passed St. Peter's Square, I spotted a nun urinating, in distress no doubt, against one of Bernini's columns. Much later I later thought about its symbolism as a feminist protest against male hierarchs. Bob Kaiser, a former Jesuit classmate, who was covering Vatican II for *Time,* chartered the car. He called me in Louvain to act as a side-kick for Robert Elson who was writing a feature article for *Life* on Pope John XXIII. It meant schmoozing my way with halting Italian into the offices of church bureaucrats to pave the way for Elson, a kindly man.

It was a rush to be snatched out of the long black line and allowed to hobnob with major journalists just before the Second Vatican

Council. At Louvain I had written a number of articles for *America* and other Catholic periodicals. One of my chief pieces was an interview with the controversial Dominican, Yves Congar, in Strasbourg. I recently found a letter he wrote. It showed a humility about his work, which was actually seminal in understanding the important place of laity in the church. Laying next to his letter was one from Jesuit Henri de Lubac, a leader of the New Theology movement. Both men were criticized by the Vatican earlier in their careers. The train trip to Strasbourg also taught me about the impossibility of sleeping on *couchettes*, three tiered slightly padded boards with mixed-sex clients. Having women in the compartment wasn't the problem. It was the unforgiving *couchettes*. The Rome visit would also give me a chance to interview Cardinal Augustin Bea, the Jesuit who headed the newly-formed Congregation for Ecumenical Relations. I've had his autographed photo on my walls since the sixties. This article also became a cover story for *America*. Such writing kept me in the sights of its editor, Thurston Davis. He would eventually offer me a job as an assistant editor.

I returned to the States in 1962 in a mood of enthusiasm and lingering tensions. I had committed myself to the priesthood in the Jesuits with the vitality of a young man. I was still idealistic enough to push aside my doubts. Experiences in Rome just before the coming ecumenical council opened up new possibilities. Bea was my hero, calling for dialogue with Protestants and other religionists. I was thinking about combining editorial work at *America* with doing a doctorate at Union Theological Seminary and Columbia University. I would be the first Catholic priest in that joint program. Vatican II was promising to pull the church into the twentieth century. I enjoyed camaraderie with fellow Jesuits. I felt accepted and respected by them. The underlying support of the wider Catholic community in the States was still buoying us up. Soon I would be celebrating a first Mass in my own parish church in Oakland where I was baptized as a child, surrounded by that immigrant population and their heirs. I want to stress the importance of the carrying power of this community support. It acted as a powerful medication to dull painful inner voices.

Yet the unresolved tensions would bubble up in quiet moments. How would I deal long term with the demands of a still semi-monastic religious life and the inner urge to acknowledge personal longings? How much was I caught up in a conceptual theology distant from my real needs? How could I adhere to the authority of a church that proclaimed unchanging doctrines in light of my new understanding of how culture had molded these ancient abstractions about the doings of God?

I came down to earth again in the countryside of Tuscany and in the province of Genova. After ordination in 1961, I visited both sides of my Italian family and celebrated Mass in the old chapel in *Pian dei Ratti*. These simpler people could still link the rituals of the church to their lives as *contadini*. I was starting to imagine spirit life more immersed in bonds of family and earth. I was viewing the church as less necessary in the eyes of God than the daily lives of people. Teilhard de Chardin had given me a much broader perspective on human development over vast eras. Such thoughts made me listen more closely to my own body-self.

1965: Gene with Jesuit superior general Pedro Arrupe at America House

4

Torn Between Work and Love

*Each of us must make his own true way, and when we do,
that way will express the universal way.*

—Suzuki Roshi

Freud summed up our life motives as love and work. The interplay of career and affection became more complex after I returned to the States. I enjoyed writing at *America* magazine and graduate study at Columbia and Union Theological Seminary. I liked teaching at Santa Clara University. But I began to fall in love with specific women along the way. This new experience, of course, conflicted with my Jesuit commitment to celibacy.

One day I would be dealing with Protestant minister intellectuals at Union who were also married. They seemed to negotiate well the worlds of heart and head, of scholarship and sexual life. Then I would return to a Jesuit community where thirteen years of training warned me about endangering my calling by listening to affective yearnings. Like Odysseus, I was on an exhilarating trip, but I saw no easy way of sailing between Scylla and Charybdis. I felt a constant tug of war.

Before *America* and Columbia, I spent a year in the last phase of Jesuit training called "Tertianship." This term meant a third year of spiritual training, involving again the thirty-day retreat according to Ignatius's Spiritual Exercises. We also ministered in hospitals and parishes. The setting of Tertianship was both odd and spectacular. Manresa Hall in Port Townsend, Washington, an old turreted mansion, had once been a hotel and would return to that status when the Jesuits sold the place some years later. The house could have been a model for Charles Addams's cartoons of witches pouring cauldrons of boiling oil on unsuspecting visitors. On a gray day it became a perfect haunted house. Yet its spectacular location near the straights of Juan de Fuca not far from the Olympic mountain ranges made it unique. Looking north the water-way led the eye to Victoria on Vancouver Island and to other small isles where we went for ministry. To the south on a good day, one could see the Olympic mountains and snow covered Hurricane Ridge. I returned to Manresa Hall recently and sensed the old vibes as I stood in the cha-pel, now a bar and lounge.

Reading my long retreat notes after forty years provides a glimpse of myself as a young priest. I understood the limited influence such a hothouse seclusion would have on my life. But I couldn't have foreseen how much my outlook would change over the years. Since Ed Flajole, our retreat director, displayed a rule-bound approach to the Exercises, I took to reading the best commentaries I could find. In my retreat jour-nal, I wrote about staying open to the Spirit, trying to make decisions as unencumbered as possible by my own narrow desires. I tried to interpret gospel stories as calls to explore inner dimensions. It's still easy enough for me to translate the language of the First Week of the Exercises concerning sin, suffering, and death into experiences of every day life. Such themes stay with me in my Buddhist-Taoist Christianity of today. Journal entries focused on letting go of self-centeredness for Christ-centeredness similar to Eastern teachings about overcoming the illusion of separate ego. The final meditation of the Exercises on gratitude for the grand cycle of God's love in creation fits in with nature mysticism, draw-ing me back to my grandfather's wine-making and vegetable garden.

Yet some convictions in my Port Townsend journals read like the writings of a stranger. Did I really believe that? There were entries on subtle understandings of Jesuit obedience in which the Holy Spirit speaks through superiors. I don't deny today that we can get valuable ad-vice from teachers and tradition. But my suspicions of authority keep me from embracing blind obedience or even "sighted" obedience. Ignatius Loyola operated in a cosmology vastly different from ours. He saw God speaking directly through the pope as the final arbiter of divine will.

Such convictions drove his missionary zeal, and that of many Jesuits, to convert non-Catholics to the true faith. This worldview takes us back to venerating the arm of Francis Xavier who baptized many Asians. Now I find such ideas foreign. At Port Townsend I was already questioning these views. I couldn't go along fully with Jesuit obedience and, especially, the need to convert others. The post- World War II period intensified the conversion ethos in the notion that all roads led to Rome. The conversion mentality expressed the needs of competitive institution-building more than the gospel of Jesus.

My long retreat journal also showed convictions about priesthood, the role of Jesus as the Christ, and the Mass that no longer make sense to me. The briefest summary of what underlay my personal religion at that time would go like this: Jesus Christ was God who came down to die on a cross to save us from our sins and lead us to heaven. The church became the continuing vehicle for this salvation history, and the Mass a ritual that represented the whole scenario. As a priest, I had special powers to make the saving sacrament of the Eucharist available and preach the gospel. (For sake of brevity, I'm leaving out the pastoral functions of the priesthood, which have to do with the compassionate care of people through their transitions and traumas. I would still hold the pastoral work of ministers to be very important.) Nor did I hold a literal reading of the classic Christian story. I didn't think that Jesus came down from some other place like the landing of a space ship from heavenly galaxies. I could make the redemptive story sound plausible, or so I thought, with sophisticated phrases.

Since all this seems to be a wholesale rejection of orthodox Christianity, I intend to revisit these themes in more detail later. I want to argue that one can legitimately be such a Christian maverick or outlier. Too many sincere Christians have been branded as heretics in church history for thinking differently. At this point, I am content to formulate two questions: how can I consider myself in any real sense a Catholic or even a Christian? And what led me to differ with classic Christian mythology?

Let me postpone answers to the first question until I have trotted out more of my life journey. The second query fits in with my experiences in graduate school at Columbia and Union Theological, as well as with my life in the *America* magazine community on 108th St. just off Riverside Park in New York City. I loved the walk up Broadway to the campuses: the bustling sidewalks, the street displays of fruit and produce, bookstores, shops of all kinds, diners, Jewish delis and coffee houses, the subterranean rumble of the subway, even the helter-skelter of cabs, and the quiet old guys sitting on benches in the middle of wide Broadway. Of course, this was pre-Starbucks. We made due with Chock-

Full-O-Nuts. I recall having coffee there with Daniel Callahan who had written a significant book on the laity and would become a leading ethicist at the Hudson Institute. I would later meet his wife, Sidney, a well-known Catholic writer, on the board of the Association for the Rights of Catholics in the Church. Andrew Greeley, a rising star, took me to the Russian Tea Room to discuss Cardinal Cody and Chicago Catholicism. I learned about the "geologist" Thomas Berry at a lively picnic with my long-time friend in Pelham Manor, Edna McCallion. I appreciated the challenging and bracing milieu.

As an assistant editor at *America*, I thought of myself as a grad student working my way through school. I wrote short commentaries and editorials as well as occasional byline articles. Of all my writings, only one seemed to disturb Cardinal Spellman's breakfast. He called my editor, Thurston Davis, to complain about my article encouraging secular dress for priests in public. Spellman loved the elaborate raiment of a Cardinal in grand liturgical style with what looks like lace and petticoats. (The piece was called "Raiment in the Space Age.") Spellman also insisted on priests wearing hats as the custom began to wane in the sixties. I was going too secular for his liking. This minor dust-up symbolizes the clash between those who clung to signs of clerical aristocracy over against the Vatican II movement toward an egalitarian people's church.

Another run-in with a Cardinal occurred when Fr. Walter Abbott, an associate editor at *America* and compiler of the documents of Vatican II, invited me to join him in a fund-raising trip to Los Angeles. We were trying to raise money for the magazine's move to the building on 56th St and Sixth Avenue. Cardinal James McIntyre greeted us in his office with scowling looks that might kill a rhinoceros. He had been going through nasty disputes with the Immaculate Heart nuns in his diocese. We must have resembled liberal lambs come to the slaughter. After excoriating us for our harmful (to the church) views at *America*, he said he wouldn't give us a nickel and hustled us out of his presence. In the hallway, Abbott and I shook our heads in dismay. It had been so much easier the day before with Bob Hope's Catholic wife. Hope himself had stopped briefly to greet us kindly.

I recently paged through my essays for *America* to find an editorial by me defending priestly celibacy in 1964. It took me by surprise since I've advocated for married and women priests for over forty years. What was I thinking? I noted that the law could be changed, but I underscored the spirituality of celibacy that I linked to Scripture: "It is the result of a long spiritual maturation in the church, meditating on the celibate witness of Christ's own priesthood. We are dealing here with a deep new Testament value . . ." The present Pope would love those lines. But I now think they are mostly wrong. We don't know whether Jesus was celibate, and the church had married priests for a millennium. I've always respected the real choice of celibacy. The mandate remains the problem. On a personal level, the piece reflects my own struggle to justify a celibate life. At thirty-four I had little contact with women, a situation that would soon change at Union Theological Seminary and, especially, at Santa Clara University.

I looked forward to my new studies at Union and Columbia. No one at the university tried to talk me out of orthodox Christian views. On the contrary, my teachers, including the sociologist of religion Thomas O'Dea with a Catholic background, accepted my clerical presence with respect. They were delighted to have a nefarious Jesuit in dialogue with the likes of Jewish historian Joseph Blau and Horace Friess of the Ethical Culture Society who introduced me to world religions. Yet it was my study of world religions and the history of religions that began to alter my view of the Christian story as I knew it up to that time.

Buddhism and Hinduism presented so much wisdom that Catholic claims to be the only way to salvation looked exaggerated. We seemed to be turning God into a narrow Judeo-Christian *paterfamilias*. Why did we need to convert these people who may have been miles ahead of us spiritually? I read Ludwig von Feuerbach, who caused a major stir in the early nineteenth century by describing a process by which we projected our experiences on to a God figure. The history of religion showed me many stories of virgin births as well as dying and rising gods such as the Isis-Osiris myth in Egypt. Such readings gave me perspective from outside the Christian camp.

Joel Steinberg, a fellow grad student at Columbia, was a mystical Jewish-Buddhist with big soft eyes and a far-away expression. He might have walked right out of a medieval Kabbalah community. Joel would invite me for tea at his dimly lit, tiny apartment with its meditation pillows and Sephardic as well as Buddhist wall scrolls. His most memorable statement actually turned out to be rather Freudian. With soulful intensity, he would look straight into my eyes and say slowly: "Gene, remember, we must always kill the fathers." It seems that I was in a slow process of doing just that.

The following memory touches my heart over half a century later. Coming out on to the corner of Broadway and 120th St. on a Saturday after engaging in library mind work, I saw Abraham Joshua Heschel, the charismatic Jewish theologian, approaching the traffic signal. He was holding two teenage girls by the hand. The look on his face was one of such joy as he turned to say hello. They were probably on their way to a Sabbath service at Jewish Theological across the street. Years later I wondered if one of the girls was his daughter, Susannah Heschel, who would become a well-known ecumenical theologian. What struck me most in this brief encounter was the silent message of this famous and holy old man smiling with two young women at his side. It was a flash of understanding about religion as being not only diverse but also grounded in the every-day-ness of life. It reminded me of the Hasidic tale that the disciple was more interested in how the rebbe tied his shoes than in the eloquence of his sermons. I've had a similar experience seeing the jubilant face of Pope John XXIII or the laughing eyes of the Dalai Lama. Authentic religion is embedded in the ordinariness of life through multiple traditions.

I took most of my courses at Union where I was excited by the ecumenical possibilities of Catholic-Protestant dialogue. My dissertation mentor, Robert Handy, renowned American church historian, advised me to write about the impact of Pope John XIII on American Protestants. It was in Handy's office during a small graduate seminar that a soft tap came on the door. Someone whispered the stunning news of John Kennedy's assassination. Indeed, we were killing the fathers in both politics and religion. Handy pulled down from his bookcases Lincoln's Second Inaugural, read sections of it, then dismissed the seminar. I can still hear the bells of James Chapel tolling as I left the hastily-called service and turned down Broadway.

Church history, with Handy and Wilhelm Pauck, gave me greater appreciation of how politics and culture shaped Christian teachings. The full divinizing of Jesus at fourth-century councils, for example, resulted from bitter, even violent disputes among Christian parties. Moreover, for political reasons, Constantine needed a unifying new god to replace traditional deities. Uniformity of religious doctrine characterized political regimes until the American and French revolutions. I wondered

what Constantine's all-powerful Christ (*pantocrator*) had to do with
Jesus of Nazareth. So culture and history became very important for
me in understanding religion. The historical approach challenged the
abstract understanding of religious doctrines. When I saw how deeply
imbued Christian teachings were by cultural and political demands, I
understood these beliefs as significantly changeable and subject to new
interpretation. This freeing of my mind excited me, especially during my
grad school time in the context of Vatican II where new windows were
being thrown open. Living in the *America* community chimed nicely
with my experience of history in the making. Important people at the
council would drop by for conversations. One of these visitors, Pedro
Arrupe, the Jesuit superior general and a hero of mine, joined us for
lively discussions. I have a commemorative picture of him as a book-
mark in one of my daily meditation volumes.

Other influences converged to alter my thinking. Daniel Day
Williams, a kindly mentor, introduced me to Process Theology. This
led me to think in an evolutionary way about religion. It gave a basis
for combining change with continuity. I've always found the title of
A.N.Whitehead's Gifford lectures, *Religion in the Making*, to be a challenging yet encouraging theme. All religions change as human consciousness develops in history. Why not a deeper development of Catholicism,
I thought, well beyond the limited ideas of John Henry Newman on the
subject in the late nineteenth century?

In the early sixties, Pierre Teilhard de Chardin occupied my mind.
The Jesuit paleontologist died in New York less than a decade before, and
was buried at the novitiate in Poughkeepsie, thanks to the intervention
of John LaFarge, the remarkable Jesuit with whom I lived at *America*.
He was the son of the famous Protestant church artist and stained glass
maker, John LaFarge. In the thirties, Jesuit LaFarge had written the first
important book on the church and the negro in America. He also drafted a never-published encyclical against anti-Semitism for Pope Pius XI.
LaFarge told me stories about his efforts on behalf of his friend, Teilhard,
who was *persona non grata* in Vatican circles for his writings on human
and earthly evolution.

Two other memories of John LaFarge stay with me. In August, 1963
he invited me to join him in Washington for the great rally where Martin
Luther King Jr. gave his "I Have a Dream" speech. I've always regretted
declining with the excuse of graduate school issues. I let books stand

in the way of my education on that one. In November of the same year, on the Sunday after Kennedy's assassination, LaFarge had gone up to his room after lunch with a New York Times section under his arm. A couple of hours later, with the house virtually empty, something moved me to knock on his door. I opened quietly to find him still in his cassock stretched out peacefully with the newspaper shaped like a tent over his feet and his reading glasses held lightly in his right hand. He had passed on. His autobiography is titled *The Manner is Ordinary*, a reference to a line from Ignatius about the life of Jesuits. I would soon be pushing further into the ordinariness of my own life.

Teilhard de Chardin's thought linked well with Process Theology. He described "the phenomenon of man," also the title of Teilhard's best known book, evolving over a vast span of time. I had trouble with Teilhard's last stage of development as "Christogenesis," which seemed too provincial. But his thinking questioned seemingly unchanging teachings of the church on creation and the understanding of Adam and Eve as well as the role of redemption through Christ. As John Courtney Murray, the Jesuit responsible for new teaching on separation of church and state at Vatican II, said during a reception for him at *America*: "Bianchi, you are becoming unstuck." At least he didn't say "unhinged." Earlier that year, we experienced the great New York blackout. I was walking out of a fitness center when the lights started to go out. Soon the city went completely dark. As I made my way on foot through honking traffic, I wondered whether my personal path in the order was growing dim. Teilhard and other thinkers were illuminating new ways for me and I was becoming more unstuck.

Yet Teilhard's pull toward spirit on earth remained cerebral. When I finished Columbia, my regional superior thought I should return to California rather than remain at *America*. He assigned me to Santa Clara University in part to temper my "doctrinaire" views. My ideas on church reform had strayed too far left. He felt that the balancing influence of a large community would trim my sails. I wasn't disappointed to leave New York, since I had been away from California for eight years. I looked forward to renewing old contacts and being closer to family. But little did my superior realize that by withdrawing me from the perils of New York, he was launching me into more dangerous terrain. I would meet three women who changed the direction of my life. I don't know if God writes straight with crooked lines, but occasionally Jesuit leaders do. From the conceptual earthiness of Teilhard, I was headed for the physical presence of women.

Santa Clara rewarded and provoked me during my two years there. I couldn't have asked for a better Jesuit community. Pat Donohoe, the university president graced the school with enlightened leadership. A number of supportive colleagues and a few eccentrics enlivened the mix. Bright and friendly students showed interest in newer approaches to religion. I enjoyed teaching, publishing and invitations to speak on radio and television. My first book on Pope John XXIII and American Protestants appeared, and I was well on my way to a second. The school backed my proposal to start a Center for the Study of Contemporary Values with a budget and space in the old Varsi library. The Center sponsored a controversial Christian-Marxist dialogue featuring the well-known American Communist, Herbert Aptheker and the French Marxist, Roger Garaudy. When the administration received complaints from alumni, President Donohoe issued an important statement about academic freedom.

But personally, thoughts of major change pressed on me. I spent the summer of 1967 in New York finishing a book in the apartment of an Episcopal priest. The time away from the routines gave me space to dwell on a recent "ah-ha" experience. I was living with students in a suite on the fourth floor of Ben Swig Hall at Santa Clara. I wanted to get out of the dark and depressing Jesuit house. One morning at first light I saw a rotund older priest in cassock and biretta walking through ground fog on his way to breakfast. He was reciting his breviary after celebrating daily Mass with a single server. The scene produced a powerful sensation in me. A voice said that I couldn't live like that into my own later years. The tableau remains as vivid forty years later as it was that day. "That" was much more than inability to say the breviary. It portrayed a life pattern that I couldn't sustain without becoming depressed and maybe sick. I thought about that vignette often as I walked around Broadway in the stifling summer heat watching kids play in open fire hydrants. For two decades I had loved the Jesuits and still appreciated their ministries. I was torn.

Another vision of sorts kept coming back to me. While a grad student at Columbia, I was invited to give a talk on ecumenism from a Catholic perspective at Lafayette College in Pennsylvania. On the bus ride, I casually read Will Herberg's *Protestant, Catholic, Jew*. Then out of nowhere I had a moving day dream. If Ignatius could start a new religious order, why couldn't I? He lived in a crucial period at the start of the modern era. Vatican II seemed to be a similar watershed for the church. I saw a new religious order of married and unmarried Jesuits joined with single and married lay people who would also be fully members. Mandated celibacy had played itself out during the last millennium. The Greyhound bus wasn't the dramatic cave at Manresa, Spain where Ignatius had his visions, nor was I as ecstatic as our Basque founder. But I felt a bodily experience with a strong sense of consolation and tears. Easy as it is to dismiss my experience as a grandiose dodge for wanting to abandon celibacy, the vision has never left me.

In a minor way, this dream came true when I left the order and became the first president of the Society of Priests for a Free Ministry (now Federation of Christian Ministries). SPFM was the first radically new priestly organization after Vatican II, not just in America but throughout the Catholic world. One could argue that nothing quite like it happened in Catholic clerical life since the Middle Ages. It inspired a number of similar movements (e.g., CORPUS) in this country and abroad. The official church reacted negatively to these groups. Such fringe efforts posed a threat to hierarchical power. They challenged it at its priestly center. Luther's rebellion in the sixteenth century was more threatening because he rejected the authority of the pope than because of his doctrinal differences with Roman theologians. Pope Leo X, who demanded that Luther recant, knew more about falcons, Renaissance art, and cuisine than he did about Christian doctrine. But the German priest's revolution threatened to undermine papal control.

These church reform ideas would have gone unheeded were it not for three women friends. I kept up with Karen, a Sister of Providence, whom I first met in Port Townsend. She was in the process of leaving her order in the late sixties. We talked about many things at her place near the University of San Francisco. I also got to know Marie at the Grail community in San Jose. Grail was an international Catholic movement of lay women who were involved in various local ministries. They fostered an ecumenical spirit working with Protestant women. A small Grail group lived near Our Lady of Guadalupe parish. A Jesuit friend at Santa Clara, Tenny Wright, introduced me to this group where we shared potluck meals and talked about changes in the church and community.

My personal tensions came to a head in late November, 1967, when I wrote in my journal: "I have resolved a deep disquiet of many years. Today I made a decision that will change the course of my life." I had taken Karen and her housemate to dinner in Santa Cruz. We conversed with honest sharing. It helped bring out issues in myself that hadn't surfaced. I decided to seek a leave of absence from the Jesuits. Then I acted like a teenager in love. I drove to San Francisco and took Karen to the beach at the west end of Golden Gate Park. I told her how I thought that she and I might join our lives. The horse was running too far ahead of the cart. She got me to slow down and said that she was already involved with a priest. I learned a lesson about projecting my mental state on to her. Karen would go on to marry and raise a family in the San Diego area. I returned to Santa Clara and drafted a letter to my superior asking to leave.

I have often given this threefold rationale to people who ask why I left, but now I put the sexual reason first. Five years after leaving I noted in my journal how uptight I had been about sexuality at that early stage. I said that I needed personal freedom. The order had on the whole treated me very well, and had given me many educational opportunities. I was grateful, I said, but now I had to risk making my own way. Santa Clara provided a liberal environment where I felt at home. But I found life in a religious order too tightly linked to hierarchical structures and strictures. The priest had no buffer between himself and the will of superiors. Moreover, I couldn't justify the dictates of Rome with the will of God. I needed to move out of the clerical system.

A second reason for leaving was the conviction that celibacy was too heavy a burden for me to carry. I wanted to relate to women in open and honest ways. I had come to realize how important this was for my overall health. Little did I realize then how many relational bumps lay on my path. Yet I couldn't continue to be celibate while no longer believing in it.

Living the priesthood in new ways formed a third motive. I was trying to reform the church's priestly lifestyles by choosing new ones, even against the will of authorities. In the spirit of the sixties, I wanted to practice a type of nonviolent dissent inside the church. I would soon write an article in *Commonweal*, "Resistance in the Church," laying out a rationale for such dissent in action. That daydream on the road to Lafayette College still motivated me. I conceived of myself as a Catholic priest at large, as it were. At that time, I didn't have some of the theological problems I now have about priestly and church claims. My spiritual cosmos would expand in ways I couldn't see.

In January of 1968 an attractive young woman walked into my class on God in Contemporary Thought. (I've wrestled with using the names of ex-wives and decided not to. I want to respect their privacy. Also I hope to speak as honestly as possible about issues between us without making these women public property. I will use an initial for each.) She had recently left the Notre Dame de Namur Sisters and was living with five other ex-nuns in a small house in San Jose. They called themselves the Fides Community. C came up after the first class and asked to audit the course. The attraction was immediate. I wanted to get to know her. I saw a tall, trim blonde in her late twenties with a playful spirit and warm smile. All my psychological projection engines went to work.

Many priests and nuns met in those hectic years of the late sixties and managed to establish enduring relationships. But some of us had impaired relational radar. Was it not having sisters, poor parental husband-wife models, lack of experience in dating? Or was it just the luck of the draw? Those are later questions that I will never finally resolve. She responded sensually as we got together many times during that celebrated and nationally ominous year. Marie, a friend of Abigail McCarthy, had gone off to help Clean Gene McCarthy battle Lyndon Johnson for the Presidency. I thought my new friend and I had a lot in common in terms of interest in church reform and a similar background in religious orders.

The year 1968 brought many emotional transitions. The rector-president of USF, Charles Dullea, threatened to cancel my summer school course on Protestant theologies as word was out about my leaving the order. I would be a source of bad example as a lame duck Jesuit. But Tom Terry, the new President of Santa Clara, said he would publicly resist such a move as academically unprofessional. USF had contracted with me to teach a course with about a hundred students enrolled. The matter died with this thrust and counterthrust. Yet it pointed out the tensions within the Jesuit community in the wake of Vatican II's unforeseen fallout. I was living in a Jesuit house for the last time. From the window of my room on Parker Avenue at USF, I could see the high school from which I entered the order and where I later taught. Most Jesuits in the San Francisco community treated me politely. A few expressed anger and disappointment. Old Lloyd Burns would not sit at a table with me. He actually got up and moved to another place in the refectory. One afternoon, as my Jesuit friend Bob Brophy, who was also about to leave, and I walked near St. Ignatius Church, Burns yelled "traitors" at us. Yet Bill Monahan, an older priest with broad, Renaissance interests, didn't miss a step in our friendship. He accompanied me to buy a used BMW for $1500 from a home garage in the Mission district. The money came from a transition subsidy given me at Santa Clara.

My own peer group in the order reacted as I expected. Most good friends like Paul Belcher, soon to become regional superior, were supportive. Paul and I would remain friends for life, taking occasions to write and visit. Other longtime friends like Ed Malatesta voiced what others might have thought. He saw my move as selfish and solipsistic. I responded that he may not have come to grips with his own feelings. I said that he had perhaps been victimized by piety and overly indoctrinated by the church. His initial reaction to a personal loss was understandable. Our relationship would mellow in later years. A former student friend at Santa Clara, Diane Quass, now a judge in Washington, D.C., helped to relieve the tension by giving me a yoyo for my birthday and flying kites with me in the hills above Los Gatos.

C and I played cat and mouse during that summer, meeting in my office for warm exchanges. I would also pick her up a few blocks from campus to avoid "scandal" as we dated. By this time our relationship had become sexual, but we didn't yet have intercourse. She was still part of a small community of ex-nuns and I was walking around campus as "Father Bianchi." We were gradually working our way out of commitments still enveloping both of us. USF had developed an outstanding summer program in theology, drawing hundreds of priests and nuns from around the country. In the high glow of Vatican II, it felt as though new doors were opening soon in the church. Even a married clergy seemed just around the corner. Many clergy and nuns dressed in secular clothes, allowing them to meld more easily into the general population on campus. In some ways, we probably reverted to teenage impulses that had been cut off during our years in religious orders. Yet that wouldn't be altogether true, since we had adult minds trying to cope with delightful, newly released emotions.

For C and me that summer gave us a time of first love with all its joy and blindness. Was it shyness or a touch of embarrassment that kept her mother, broom in hand, sweeping off the front door threshold when C first introduced me? In hindsight, she may have been trying to slow us down a bit. Her mother worked with the Catholic Legion of Decency, which censored movies. It must have seemed odd for her newly ex-nun daughter to be dragging her priest lover to such a decent Catholic front door. But parents, on the whole, were remarkably flexible. It wasn't long before her large clan embraced us as an item. The laity, with concrete experience of the ups and downs of marriage, was miles ahead of the hierarchy in accepting love affairs among religious professionals.

I worried that my mother would be very upset by my leaving the Jesuits. Although she wasn't a regular churchgoer (blaming Gino for "getting mad" if she went to Mass; Gino, the Furious, was a convenient excuse for many things.), Katie took pride in my status as a successful Jesuit. It was something like "my son, the doctor," for a Jewish mother. "My son, the Jesuit professor," worked just as well for a working-class Catholic mother. Now she would have to face the Jesuit Mothers Club with some feigned sadness in their looks, as just another mother disgraced by her wayward son unable to control his sexual instincts. And then she had to contend with less sophisticated neighbors at the corner grocery store. Rumors buzzed in the streets. Have you heard about Katie's boy? And what would the daily communicants like Mary Bozzini say?

But my mother's distress over my leaving went deeper than what the neighbors would say. She was at heart a deeply religious person shaped in the Catholic tradition. She saw the priesthood as a high calling. In her mind the priest stood closer to God, to holy things. In indefinable ways, I had fallen. I had ceased to be as good a boy as she (and God) wanted. How could there not be disappointment and covert reproach in her mixed feelings? My brother came to the rescue as we presented my decision. He was at his lawyerly best in helping her understand new changes in the church and my own personal needs. Gino, of course, took it all quite well. His concern was how I was going to make a living at the ripe age of thirty-eight. George explained that I had a job at Emory University and that they would actually pay me to teach religion. I credit my parents' Italian heritage for a more humane acceptance of my leaving. Italian Catholics respected priests, but they avoided the Jansenism and legalism that affected Irish Catholics. Jansenism had to do with rigid attitudes about sex. Legalism concerned hard and fast laws whose observance determined heaven or hell in the next life. The Italian attitude of *ci arrangiamo*, "we'll work it out," spilled over to religion. God will understand our human frailties. Italians were close enough to ecclesiastical power not to take it too seriously. The Irish, in their perennial battles against English heretics and political dominance, couldn't take Vatican power seriously enough. There was the occasional horror story. Parents of a friend who left the priesthood cut off all communication with him and his wife. Christmas cards and presents from them were thrown into the basement unopened.

By the time I headed my insecure BMW over the Sierras on the long trip to Emory University and the deep South, I was in a new phase of flux. A memorable incident near Lake Tahoe symbolized my internal state. I noticed that the engine was losing power on steep grades. When I pulled into a service station, a mechanic looked under the hood. We couldn't believe our eyes. An important locking screw that helped to contain the car's compression had come loose and fallen to a precarious ledge on the engine. I had driven miles with that loose bolt sitting on a precipice. Why didn't it fall out on to the road? I, too, was on an exhilarating trip, but unsure about my own power to pull it off. Many intellectual challenges eroded my theological security. Yet the same acids of mind opened new vistas.

Through Bill Monahan, I spent my last days in California at artist Louisa Jenkins's house in Carmel, a Frank Lloyd Wright-like dwelling. Here I read *Humanae Vitae*, Pope Paul VI's letter condemning birth control. This encyclical confirmed my decision to leave the official priesthood. The Pope held to a hopelessly outdated teaching, while he rejected the majority views of the commission he established to advise him. When C saw me off from a house she was sitting in Palo Alto in late August, 1968, I saw myself as a reform-minded priest who had newly awakened to body and earth. C and I had recently done a four day session on sensory awareness at Grace Cathedral in San Francisco.

I also told my superior that I would continue to celebrate Mass, even though I wasn't supposed to during my two-year leave of absence. I wrote in my journal: "I will not play the laicization game, which I think is bad theology. It plays into the hands of those who don't want to see new lifestyles for priests. We have to demonstrate the new way by celebrating Mass in our new condition." And I wrote on another page: "I must hold on to the vision I have for priesthood and church, even against ecclesiastical opposition. We will prevail." Looking back, I see some self-referential heroics in those claims. But, after all, the year of Martin Luther King Jr.'s assassination rang with refrains of "We Shall Overcome." How could I not hear it?

1971: GENE WITH *BARBA GIANNI*
AT THE "CHAPEL OF THE CHICKEN HOUSE"

5

New Hopes and Dark Night

Love winter when the plant says nothing.

—Thomas Merton

The Fourth of July, 1969, began a new phase of discovery and disappointment. C and I ran under the sailing rice to our borrowed TransAm, leaving behind the wedding party in her sister's garden in Saratoga, California. My Baptist theologian friend Jim McClendon, assisted by a former Jesuit Dick Pfaff, had just officiated at a lovely outdoor ceremony. When I now look at photos of family and friends standing in that sun-drenched setting, I think about the uncertainties of our comings and goings. Our choices on that day seemed so meant-to-be. We shared common backgrounds, strong feelings for one another, and similar expectations: the ex-nun marries the ex-priest, a much repeated pattern in those years. Even the *Atlanta Constitution* and *Time* would eventually play the story as an example of the new Catholicism.

We weren't traveling very far that afternoon, only to the beach at Santa Cruz for a brief honeymoon. It was an independence day for both of us. We had freed ourselves from the confines of religious orders. We were adults who should have been able to scope out ways to live together, even though we were stumbling novices at sex in those early days by the sea. We knew the nervousness would pass with good will on both sides, and it did. But for all our seeming adulthood, we had not explored those dark places easily neglected by church professionals. Through the ups and downs of this marriage, I learned things that I didn't experience in Jesuit life. Marriage to C became a catalyst for knowing negative aspects of myself that I could hide in the order.

Some men by temperament or luck can avoid facing parts of themselves they don't like. They might be upset within, but they can cloak outward expression of face to face anger, unkindly expressed judgments, and sullen passive aggressiveness. Yet if we look at Dante's *Divine Comedy* as symbolic of our journeys, descent into inferno seems to be a prerequisite to self-understanding. If we lop off that third of his story, the human comedy would surely be less divine. It was no fun for the poet to follow Virgil down those infernal rungs, but would he have been ready for Beatrice without that trip? Or can we realize the advice of Socrates, "Know thyself," without grappling with our inner furies?

Marriage also taught me something about confronting unpredictability. We can't predict life, even in religious orders. But such groups remove much tension arising from uncertainty. Jesuits have full material and medical support from first vows to death. Dictates of superiors can inject a degree of job uncertainty, but members of the order enjoy a permanent safety net. Such a life provides a steady platform for service and learning. Yet facing unpredictability induces humility about our ability to control things.

After a few years at Emory, academic tenure brought an important dimension of stability for me, but my relations with women were destabilizing. I didn't want it to turn out this way, but my bumpy road through three marriages brought a mixed blessing. I emphasize "mixed" because I contributed to the unhappiness of my wives, and these experiences distressed me. Yet these events put me in touch with failure on a personal level.

My years with C were the most topsy-turvy time of my life. I never became a sixties flower child or a radical like Abbie Hoffman. I was a liberal, ex-Jesuit academic who taught religion at Emory University. A stressed marriage cracked the relatively steady state of my life, pushing me to inner explorations and questionable sexual experiments. At the same time, I had assumed leadership roles among resigned priests who were leaving in large numbers. As first president of the Society of Priests for a Free Ministry (SPFM), I wrote and spoke on a national stage about the need for a married clergy and women priests. I also conducted small group liturgies in friends' homes. All of these activities put me at odds with the Catholic hierarchy as a renegade.

Anti- (Vietnam)War actions and travels with C in a 1959 largely windowless VW van roughly converted into a traveling bedroom (my mother called it "their hippie wagon") kept me in contact with many who challenged authority. In the fall of 1969, we drove to Washington for the protest march around Nixon's White House. We combined such trips with meetings for SPFM and contacts with active priests who supported changes in the church. Moreover, Emory University at this time was slowly coming out of its patrician-plantation contentment. Blind patriotic obedience to military ventures (reminiscent of blind obedience in religious orders) was crumbling. Students cut class to march across campus chanting "Hell no, we won't go!" against the draft. Our southern school kicked ROTC off campus. Activist professors like Jack Boozer in my department had long been in the forefront of racially integrating Emory. Slow rocking on verandas sipping bourbon and water, commenting on the price of cotton and those damn Yankees, was long gone in Atlanta. Add to all this the growth of my good-looking salt-and-pepper beard and we have the tableau of a low-profile rebel.

Yet in all this change, the center of the storm swirled around life with C. When things were good, she was very sexually attractive to me. Unfortunately, other men thought so, too. She wanted to explore things at every turn, from pottery-making to the grind of law school. Her critics called her a dilettante with deep personal insecurities. These traits were part of the picture, but her playful flair was a lovely counterweight to my seriousness. Without her I would probably never have sat "On the Dock of the Bay" with Marvin Gaye or felt the rhythms of musical luminaries from the Beatles to Santana who were defining the sentiments of an epoch and playing in our 1920s brick bungalow.

During our first year together, we rented one side of a frame two-bedroom duplex in Decatur, a community near Emory University. Our landlady, Mrs. Rice, a divorcee, lived next door. She was a simple, middle-aged woman with big hair that shot straight up. She smoked a lot and was very concerned about bugs, which she pronounced "buuugs" in a guttural drawl from southern Alabama. This entomological obsession didn't blight her personality. She was usually upbeat and liked to sip bourbon on the rocks alongside her backyard swimming pool. She enjoyed that touch of class: living in blue collar Decatur with the luxury of an oversized in-ground pool. C got her first instructions on cooking a Thanksgiving turkey from Mrs. Rice, and she never complained about noises from our bedroom separated from hers by paper thin walls.

For all her charms, and for me they were many, C was a very unsettled person. This may sound like my excuse for a failed marriage. I also risk appearing as the professorial pedant. Yet a friend characterized her as a lovely butterfly flitting from flower to flower. She sought novelty and stimulation. Yet that was part of her attraction over against my workaholic personality. Her freshness was both appealing and exasperating.

She left home after Catholic high school to join the Notre Dame de Namur nuns, a conservative group, at a time when many young women were entering convents in the early sixties. The sisterhood gave her a decent college education (she majored in art) and a stable community, although the roller coaster changes of Vatican II were just around the corner. The move from the complete body cover of the Namur nuns with only face and hands peeping out of black wool and starched head piece to lay clothes symbolized a psychic revolution among religious women.

As the next to last of a long string of siblings, she probably didn't receive enough emotional support from undemonstrative parents. Her father, Jim, was a classic example of the self-made engineer, a success story in Oakland after coming up from rugged rural poverty in Minnesota. Like many men in his generation, he displayed affective distance. With an iron will, he stopped smoking cold turkey in his fifties. Her mother, Mary, was a kind but moralistic person. But parental influences may have counted less than her genetic make-up. In trying times, I would comment (part of my unhelpful judgmental tendencies) on C's before-drinks and after-drinks personality. Alcoholic problems affected others in her clan.

Her new home in the convent kept C from experiencing the mating games of fellow twenty-year-olds. Now this pretty and unsure blonde was coming out into the maelstrom of the late sixties where excitement not stability was the cultural marker. She felt good about getting a job with the Model Cities program in Atlanta. Eventually she would work for the Department of Family and Child Services. These involvements with the poor appealed to her altruism and her concern for disadvantaged blacks. The jobs gave her a sense of accomplishment. On the artistic side, she bought a pottery wheel from an artist friend, and set it up in a back room of our house. We were developing circles of friends in Atlanta, a number of them former priests and their wives or couples we got to know at Emory's Newman Center. We socialized with them and occasionally did home liturgies together. There was our ill-fated investment with a former priest in pizza parlors in Carrollton, Georgia. My brother told me not to worry: "if all you lose in life is three thousand dollars, count yourself lucky," he said.

Former Trappist Anselm Atkins and his ex-Carmelite wife, Margaret Kavanaugh, built a house in the round not far from our duplex. I could only watch in awe at the energy of these brave souls pouring their own foundations. Anselm was remarkable in other ways: writer, stained glass maker, naturalist (his house was a small natural-history museum), and published atheistic humanist. I looked forward to our conversations about Darwin over pizza and beer near his enameled Danish wood-burning stove. Therapists Sarah Lopez and Frank Ostrowski, another former Catholic clergyman, were our earliest friends in Atlanta. Sarah met C in a pottery class. Frank has been an admirable peacenik in his involvements with Fellowship of Reconciliation. In very recent years, he has become a wonderful model of dignity and courage in dealing with cancer. Richard Roesel and Dana Greene, graduate students at Emory, would remain supportive friends especially during my relational problems. After long careers in the D.C. area, they returned to the Emory community. A few years ago, I used my real estate skills to find them an Atlanta home.

The Religion Dept. at Emory University became a source of stability for me during marital crises and a supportive environment for academics. We avoided the factional battles of other departments where young professors were driven to side with one or other party. I was receiving good teaching reviews from students and critical encouragement from senior colleagues about moving toward tenure. I managed by grace and luck to find the right job in a fine place. Emory has become one of the top schools nationally in religious studies. It was a blessing to be paid to do what I liked to do: teach and write.

In the graduate program, we collaborated with the larger faculty of the Candler School of Theology. While there was some friction between the Religion Dept. and Candler, the partnership prospered. Graduate teaching allowed me to explore special areas of interest like psychology and religion. I cherished friendships with Candler colleagues and graduate students. Specialty courses, such as autobiography and spirituality, turned out to be ways for me to deal with personal challenges. For example, during my emotional crisis when C left, I went into therapy with a Jungian analyst, David Garrett, in the Bay Area. This experience led me to study Carl Jung more fully and develop a seminar on his thinking with graduates.

Emory College had a big enough program in religious studies so that I could teach courses that held academic and personal interest. A course in Process Theology developed because of the intellectual importance for me of approaching the history of religions with an adequate philosophical outlook. It helped to make sense of change in traditional religions that clung to unchangeable teachings. Later I would start a course on death and dying as I faced a midlife crisis with the collapse of my first marriage. My teaching and books on aging were a natural sequel to the death-and-dying course. In a sense, I backed into aging from the topic of death. These forays into psychology, death, and aging had both an intellectual and personal focus. On the academic side, they represented my attempts to think about religion in metaphorical ways, pertaining to life as actually lived. Jung helped me to both open up the shadow side of my personality and think about religion as powerful myths and rituals. I tell people now, as I live my own final season, that I have moved from doing library work on death and aging to my own laboratory study.

Another course I initiated at Emory on man-woman liberation and religion brings out the interplay between personal life and academia. C embraced the new women's movement, keeping her family name after our marriage. She associated with feminists who were trying to equalize home chores with their husbands or partners. Her women friends were reading Betty Friedan and moving into the work world. C was in full rebellion from both her authoritarian father and from an autocratic male-dominated church. I remember putting both of our last names on the mail box and writing an article about that experience for *National Catholic Reporter*. I agreed with the aims of the women's movement, and saw it as part of a wider liberation from forms of social oppression.

In the early seventies, Rosemary Ruether and I collaborated on one of the first books on this topic from theologians, *From Machismo to Mutuality*. It expressed our own changing experiences on the importance of feminism for church and society. Yet these same positive energies fed into rationalizations contributing to the failure of our marriage. Of course, feminism didn't have to go in this direction. Many marriages incorporated its themes in beneficial ways. But we were naïve enough to think that our relationship could sustain the tensions of multiple partners.

Up to this point, I've talked about marriage with C and my new academic life at Emory. I was also involved in Catholic reform movements, and we participated in activities against the Vietnam war. It was a time of decisions, sometimes questionable ones, for myself in face to face situations. I couldn't simply fall back on the Jesuits or on the wisdom of the church. Marriage, university life, a church shaken by Vatican II, and the insane killings of Vietnam threw us off-balance. Old ways were dying, while new lifestyles seemed to be right around the corner. Although a few years older than the hippie generation, I shared much of its spirit for questioning authority.

The Catholic Church shaped an important part of our backgrounds. In our first two years of marriage, we maintained this common interest. We talked about needed changes in the church and how we might make a difference. We hosted liturgies with friends in our living room, participated in Masses at the Newman Center, engaged in ecumenical university worship services and stayed in touch with many Catholics who kept alive the still vibrant spirit of Vatican II. Pope Paul VI disappointed us by upholding the birth control teaching that no longer made sense. His 1968 encyclical began a forty-year policy of retrenchment at the Vatican, a pulling back from the spirit of Vatican II on many levels.

Through life with C, I also realized the liturgy of bodily life. It became as important as any Sunday Mass. I remember a pillow conversation we had waking up on a bright spring morning in our old house on Emory Circle with birdsong coming through open windows, our bodies touching closely, Savanarola, our black-and-white cat, walking over our legs, and a sense of connection with it all. We agreed that this communion was equal in holiness to the house liturgy we were to attend later that morning.

The celibacy issue for priests seemed solvable within a reasonable amount of time. Priests were leaving in large numbers. In a television interview with David Susskind, former Maryknoller Eugene Kennedy and I spoke about the benefits of optional celibacy for Catholicism. We projected a new era, far different from the conditions that brought about mandated celibacy in the Middle Ages. Feudal barons no longer stole church property to hand it on to their priest sons. Moreover, the Catholic theology of sex, we said, was finally liberating itself from the

Manichean negatives of two millennia. Sexual involvement had been associated with the sinful body rather than with corporeal sacrament. In the new thinking, God was as present in physical loving. The church pew was no longer the antithesis of the conjugal bed.

I had been elected first president of the Society of Priests for a Free Ministry. Former clerics Tom Durkin, Ed Best, Rocco Caporale, Bill Manseau, and others launched a new movement in the church. We thought that it wasn't enough to petition for change. We took a page from Martin Luther King Jr. and Saul Alinsky about the need for organized action. We saw it as civil disobedience in the church, urging priests who left to continue celebrating the Eucharist and perform other ministries. The growing shortage of priests, we argued, produced an emergency situation for Catholics that justified our public ministries.

These services would be free from outmoded hierarchical laws and free to fulfill people's pastoral needs. We were of two minds. We wanted to keep open lines of communication with bishops, but SPFM was also an in-your-face operation. A few years later, a Vatican Congregation condemned our extra-canonical activities. By 1973, SPFM had developed a wider vision. Changing its name to Federation of Christian Ministries, it cultivated the ministry of women as equals in the church. The word "priests" in the SPFM title identified in people's minds with men. FCM issued one of the first calls for the ordination of women in the Catholic Church. Women in FCM could also be certified for all ministries, including the celebration of the Eucharist.

If we fast-forward to 1994, my present wife, Peggy, and I were relaxing in a *pensione* not far from the Vatican where we read Pope John Paul's document forbidding even the discussion of women priests in the church. The pope tried to turn his views about women's ordination into an absolute matter of faith. He returned to the strange anatomical argument that Jesus was a male, and therefore, anatomically incorrect women could not be priests. Oddly enough, this approach echoes the church's biological argument against the use of contraceptives. Both positions rest on a kind of biological determinism. In one case, no penis, no ordination; in the other, no condom should interfere with natural body functions. The Pope also invoked church tradition, which, he said, did not accept women priests. A male-dominated system resorted to physical arguments rather than look at cultures that produced male rule.

Recent scholarship shows that women in the early church presided at eucharistic celebrations.

I was excited to continue my life as a teacher and priest after I resigned from the official clergy. My SPFM role kept me in the forefront of efforts for change. I could voice the desires of thousands of resigned priests who wanted to continue their ministries within the church. I addressed the National Federation of Priests Councils, then under the leadership of Frank Bonnike, who would soon leave and marry. We met with representatives of the national bishops' conference and the major superiors of religious men. In San Francisco I brought the vision of SPFM to the Catholic Theological Society of America. Our movement divided priests of good will. Some saw it as excessive and disobedient. Others praised us as a prophetic voice. When I met with Cardinal Leo Suenens, a Belgian progressive at Vatican II, at the Grace mansion in Manhasset, he urged us to continue our work without going into detail about our controversial ministries. Knowing that the church was in a state of flux, he wanted to keep priests working within it.

I shouldn't exaggerate in presenting SPFM as a major player in ongoing struggles with the Vatican. In Rome's eyes, we were failed priests whining at mother church, renegades who would not go quietly into the "lay state," men who wanted active sexual lives. We were unable to sacrifice animal passion for God's sake, as they, the good priests, had done. Rome saw us as scandalizing the laity. The paternalistic penchant, so powerful in hierarchical circles, envisions the laity as naïve children. It's amazing how this attitude continues even today among the newly minted, French-cuffed younger priests who view the laity as spiritual minors. The hierarchy classified SPFM as a Catholic version of Hindu untouchables.

Yet themes of women's liberation were much easier to cope with in the abstract. Living with C in all its complexity was something else. Over the first two years, we unpacked the baggage of our lives, trying to fit it into a viable marriage. Some of that stuff was easily seen while other parts were hidden. Neither of us were hair-on-fire church lefties, although we shared strong anti-war sentiments about Vietnam. We supported Jane Fonda who spoke at Quaker House near Emory before her trip to Hanoi. With some personal unease, I stood on a soap box, Hyde Park style, in front of the student center at lunch time exhorting passersby to resist the war.

On a very cold November day, we marched around Nixon's White House to protest the war. I shared the podium with Andrew Young at peace rallies in Atlanta, and I won an election to be one of four Georgia delegates-at-large for George McGovern at the Miami Democratic convention in 1972. These pursuits stemmed from research for my third book, *The Religious Experience of Revolutionaries*, and from a growing interest in religion and violence. This was the focus of my research during a Berkeley sabbatical that became a major transition time in our marriage. The exact event of this watershed was seeing Liv Ullman in "Scenes from a Marriage." My heart dropped after the movie when C, in a coffee shop on College Ave., said how much she identified with the dissatisfied Ullman figure.

Our annual treks to California were fun for both of us. Since C craved variety, the long journey west in our hippie wagon was usually upbeat. Making love after lunch in that oddly-built vehicle was memorable. We would have to find a secluded spot, pull the shade on our single back window, face the van into thick growth, and assume positions that would have make a contortionist proud. Night time provided more cover, but by then we were generally too tired for anything but sleep. Most nights we stayed at campgrounds, but occasionally we would venture more bizarre arrangements, like the night we stayed in the parking lot of Las Vegas's Riviera Hotel Casino. We availed ourselves of the hotel bathrooms, and wandered around that surrealistic gaming world.

We both enjoyed contacts with family and friends in the Bay Area. We wanted to come back west, but that meant finding a teaching job. As the economy of the early seventies took a dip, I job-hunted from Eureka to Monterey. I even looked into a state job in educational administration in Sacramento. I searched the Catholic old-boy networks of longtime friends. The go-west job pursuit put new pressure on us. I was hesitant to leave Emory, especially after getting tenure in 1972. It would have been very hard to find a teaching-research situation to match what I had.

One summer C was so discouraged about returning south that she gave me an ultimatum: she would give Atlanta another year and would then come west with or without me. My best option to relocate came in 1974 when I was invited to be Distinguished Visiting Professor at Sacramento State University. I also taught courses at University of California, Davis. I put great energy into making it work for the long run, but school budgets were shrinking. My conservative brother, whose own marriage was on the skids, advised me to hold on to Emory. "Watch out for those damn fanciful boondoggles," he said. George was distinctly anti-New Age. "What the hell was I doing at Esalen?" he would ask in his critical mode. His manner remains the antithesis of Carl Rogers's non-directive therapy. He would sum things up, quoting the immortal line of our *contadino* father, Gino Bianchi Gino: "Keepy you central nerve straight, Biggie Boy; no bullishite."

Keeping my central nerve straight wasn't easy as C and I struggled with our relationship. If we imagine marriage breakdown as a circle, changes at the periphery point to deeper issues. C's interest in the Catholic Church and organized religion had faded. The ethos of the sixties, feminism in particular, pulled her in radical directions. She could no longer see the male-dominated church making life better for people whether that had to do with poverty in the slums or rules about sexual behavior. I still worked with reformist Catholic groups. Moreover, the university environment was not to her liking. She appreciated individuals in academia, but she found intellectual life too abstract. With some smart counseling and a measure of good will, we might have negotiated problems on the circumference of the circle, if the inner zones had been healthier.

Closer to the center of our breakdown were the face to face negativities. We undermined the wells of mutual affection by badly handled fights. Conflict is normal in marriage, but when feelings harden into fixed positions, they degenerate into angry disrespect. Prospects for repairing the breach lessen. My journals show a litany of my shortcomings in her eyes: too controlling, not able to listen, lack of respect for women, too judgmental, too driven by career to pay attention to emotional needs. She was in some measure right. Then there was my list of her defects: unable to grow up and settle down, lack of inner confidence that kept her jumping from one thing to another, uncritical acceptance of feminism, demanding, playing the child to my adult. These complaints are not relationship killers in themselves. Yet their tone and intensity, like a stream cutting through its foundation, gradually undermine the union.

Two and a half years into our marriage C began seeing other men. After years of seclusion in a convent, she was discovering herself as a "foxy lady." After these early encounters, R came into her life. As a black who worked his way up from the ghetto to social worker, he seemed to have a kind of sensual attractiveness that I lacked. She saw him as a free spirit like herself. He had a knack for responding to women, she said. R was also married to a beautiful black woman. "Gene, I really love you," C would say, "you're my main man, but we can't let the rigid ways of the past keep us from having a second man."

It was, after all, the age of Aquarius. How could I, who taught a course on man-woman liberation, not go along with this Main-Man philosophy? Wasn't it just a reverse version of an old European tradition of men having mistresses? It's hard to unravel the thoughts that induced me to embrace her new ways. In part, it was a naïve hope that "Main-Manism" could work for us. But at another level, I feared that she would leave me if I didn't ride this out. At least it was a way of not having to face rejection, public embarrassment and loneliness.

During a sabbatical year in Berkeley, I did research on religion and violence. C threw pots while she waited for word about getting into Emory's law school. She sold her pottery at weekly street fairs on Telegraph Ave. I remember my feeling of regret when she told me that I had never come to see her throw a pot in Berkeley. We talked about having a child, but she said she had body fears about pregnancy and couldn't deal with a baby in law school. She was considerably upset when a delayed period made us think she might be pregnant. But she probably had an intuition that she was too unsettled and that I was not the right person.

During this Berkeley stay, I ran into a lovely woman I had known in my Jesuit student days at Union Theological. She was married to a minister, but that relationship had become very rocky. Here was a chance to experience "Main-Womanism." C, who kept up correspondence with her Atlanta man-friend, said okay. But I wasn't very good at it. Was it the impact of C's dual allegiance or my own lack of brain-penis coordination? I was always too nervous with new women. This made me jealous of the Lothario qualities of friends who seemed to be sexual Olympians. I found myself virtually impotent via premature ejaculation with new lovers. Such a curse. The pattern repeated itself between marriages. Perhaps my superego, shaped by mother, Katie, and the church, blocked my desired performance while experimenting with "Main-Womanism."

Although I haven't put much store in astrology, I had a reading at a large fair at UC Davis. I phoned my mother to ask her about the exact hour of my birth: "O, Eugene, you don't believe in that nonsense (my im-

age of the good boy priest was slipping rapidly) after all your education."
But she did give me the hour. The reading was interesting: you will have
trouble with women. You are a writer, but you hold back, not letting it
all hang out. The battle of Taurus and Aquarius seemed to be coming
full circle.

After a psychosynthesis workshop at Esalen, I came to see "sub-
personalities" pushing and pulling in my mind. These aspects of myself
came alive with great intensity in the final event of our separation. While
I was teaching at Sacramento State, C met a man at a party in Atlanta.
This black architect swept her away. I mention "black" here and previously because all her lovers were African Americans. My fantasy mind
told me that I could never give her the kind of experience she got from
these men. In the words of our friend, Sarah Lopez, I was the thesis for
C, her earlier man-friend the antithesis and the architect the synthesis.
In theory (because their marriage would also collapse), the architect
combined my smarts and status with the other man's winning sexual
aggressiveness (C's words). Yet maybe the comment of my gay next door
neighbor, Julian, cut to the chase. A master of southern drawl, he could
turn one syllable words into two or three. It sounded like this: "Geeanne,
you just caan't leave that girill aloanne." He was referring to my long
absence in Sacramento.

C's visit during the Christmas holidays of 1974 became both emotional rollercoaster and bombshell. During the first part of the two week
visit, she seemed excited to be back with me. She was sexually respon-
sive, and even wanted us to buy a plot of vacation land near Truckee.
Then one Sunday she seemed very depressed. I asked her what was
happening. She asked for a separation. She saw too many gaps in our
relationship mainly because I was not able to fulfill her emotional needs.
She said that she felt bad to have needed the first man's support, but she
resented my hostility toward him. To her I was venturesome in thought,
but hesitant in decision-making. She portrayed herself as an extroverted
person wanting to taste variety. I felt miserable, but I wondered if she
was just venting. We had had similar tension-releasing talks before. Yet
this time I sensed a note of certainty in her voice. She tried to soften the
news, saying that I would find someone better suited to me, someone
who would give me children.

Powerful feelings of loss and fear of being alone pressed down on
me. I said that I loved her and wanted to grow old with her. But later I re-

membered a framed statement in a woman friend's home in Sacramento: "Unless I can feel in my gut what it means to be truly alone, I will never be free." When I meditated on this, I felt some peace. It was an invitation to face what I feared most: rejection and abandonment, and a challenge to find resources to live out of that experience. It took forty-four years for me to finally encounter a dark night of the soul that came unbidden and unwanted. Nothing in my Jesuit life so gripped my inner core. But no personal relationship in the order could match my commitment to C. Rejection at this level pushed me into depression. I saw a psychiatrist who prescribed lithium. The drug made me feel like a zombie who was wandering around with the spaced-out sensation of viewing the world from an alien planet. One morning I decided to throw away the pills, shave off my beard and resort to counseling and meditation. For some reason mornings were always harder to deal with than later times of day. But my decision to embrace psycho-spiritual practices gave me new energy.

I would still alternate between new vigor, sadness, and anger. When C got back to Atlanta, after a visit with the architect in LA, she called to say that she was going to live with him. I was mad and felt betrayed. After talking with my theologian friend Jim McClendon, I flew to Atlanta without telling her I was coming. I told her that she was acting like an impulsive child, not wanting to work out our marriage commitment in therapy. I said she was deceived by the romantic glow with a glamorous guy. She had told me that he met her at the LA airport in a flashy Audi with the latest pop music on the tape deck. I wanted to say that she was self-deceived, that she needed to get in touch with the insecurity that kept her flitting from one job and one man to another. Whatever truth resided in these judgments, they were ultimately ways for me to justify myself and feel righteous.

On a cold winter morning at Evan's Fine Foods near Emory, we had a final breakfast together. She expressed much appreciation for me, saying that she didn't want to lose me. I could see that there was no stopping her from going to LA. The only hope for our marriage at this point was to let her go. She said that if she returned, we would do therapy together, build a new relationship and have a child. I would see C only two more times: once at the divorce session in Sacramento, sadly waving her off in a newer VW camper that had carried us on many good trips, and once more in San Francisco. When I was on vacation in North Carolina in

1984, I got word that she had died in San Luis Obispo, after being found alone and unconscious by a nephew. She and the architect were then separated. They said she was carrying my picture in her wallet.

1972: Georgia delegate
to Democratic National Convention, Miami

6

Old Patterns and Hard Learning

Make your ego porous. Will is of little importance,
complaining is nothing, fame is nothing.
Openness, patience, receptivity, solitude is everything.

—RAINER MARIA RILKE

WOULDN'T IT BE GOOD if we could just take the insights from our best meditations or therapy sessions and turn them into reality? Yet we can only do that in a kind of Walter Mitty flight of imagination where we turn ourselves quickly into saints and bodhisattvas. But the hard reality of our embodied self, steeped in genetic proclivities and social environments, doesn't allow such magic-wand solutions. We rise a bit only to fall back into well-grooved patterns. Two steps forward, one and a half steps back. But even this halting progress on the path is more than acceptable from a Zen point of view where our imperfect personalities are just fine when embraced in moments of meditative insight.

So, too, from a Christian perspective, our deepest personal roots go beyond our concepts. They exist in a "cloud of unknowing." The medieval treatise by that name was, after all, authored by "anonymous," indicating that the names we give ourselves and our self-estimates fall away when we connect with the divine in stillness. But when I returned to Atlanta in late 1975, I still didn't understand this paradoxical alchemy, the polarity between my efforts and the letting go of all striving in contemplative moments. The Jesuits had given me a key to such alchemy in the order's mottos, "contemplative in action" and "finding God in all things." But incorporating these ideals in my world of love and work would keep me on a bumpy road.

After seven years of trying to relocate my career in California, I was gradually making peace with life at Emory and in Atlanta. It's hard to sort out motivations for this change of heart. I no longer had the tug of C wanting to return west, and I realized the limits of the job market on the Pacific coast. I had turned forty-five, and as I would learn later in my studies of aging, I was unconsciously beginning to count my years from the end rather than from the beginning. Time for new ventures was not on my side. But from a positive standpoint, I appreciated more fully what I had at Emory and in my circle of Atlanta friends.

Religious studies at Emory increased in quality and the university was on the cusp of a quantum leap in expansion. Soon our faculty in Judaic studies would grow by two or three positions. Not long after that we hired experts in Indian and other Asian traditions. Cognate departments hired scholars on Islam and the Near East. Interdisciplinary work both in research and in the classroom was catching on at Emory. By the end of the decade, the Woodruff Foundation would give the school one of the largest single donations in American educational history, over a hundred million dollars. For all this, I thought it worth putting up with the heat and humidity of Atlanta. And the city itself was growing more cosmopolitan in population, restaurants, the arts, and in its general mentality.

On a deeper level, Emory pleased me because I was enjoying more fully my vocation as a teacher. This calling is much more than having a degree or being called "Professor" or "Doctor." Of all the careers I could have followed, being a teacher/writer was the most intimately connected to what I'd call my soul's choice. Teaching spoke to an affinity between who I was and what I was meant to be. I loved to explore the history of ideas and spiritual movements in dialogue with students and colleagues. Like Socrates, I had found the right marketplace to wander about asking questions and attempting answers. Even modest pay sufficed if I could do what I really wanted. Yet it took the turmoil of divorce and renewed self-questioning about my vocation to bring this home to me. During the California maelstrom of my failed marriage with C, my good Jesuit friend, Paul Belcher, counseled me to get in touch with my calling from within.

David Garrett, a Jungian analyst in El Cerrito, a suburban community just north of Berkeley, helped me see the direction of my dream imagery in a similar light. There was the recurrent Jesuit dream where

I was torn between staying in the order and leaving. The "oughts" and habits of the past pulled against the Jesuit-inspired quest to move in new directions. The most memorable of these Jesuit dreams was quite dramatic. In a large stone seminary at the top of a hill, I went around debating whether I should stay or leave the order. At night I would steal down the hill to visit a lover in her small wooden cabin. On the descent, I stumbled over rocks while threatening dogs growled and tore my cassock. After the tryst, I would climb back up the steep hill, but the animals were quiet and gave me safe passage. Beyond the clear sexual aspects of the dream, it denotes a life pattern of belonging (or wanting to belong) and not belonging. This non-belonging or partial belonging underscores how I feel about the order and the Catholic Church to this day. I'm sure it also relates to other aspects of my life.

After my return to Emory, my underlying vocation of teacher/ priest (not in a cultic sense but in that of the care of souls) continued with less splitting between mind and body. Garrett and I had discussed a series of "Henry Kissinger" dreams. I was questioning the worth or power of my calling as a teacher in contrast to what seemed to be real power in the world. But such longings would be contradicted by the peach seed dream: finding that core within that could give me true consolation about continuing on the path chosen. Odd, too, that my quest should take place in the peach state of Georgia. In making life decisions, Ignatius Loyola urged spiritual seekers to listen closely to what he called consolations of the spirit. In the end, it reflected what my Louvain Jesuit counselor André Hayen said about himself in an essay he wrote upon leaving the order to marry at age seventy. He spoke about tapping into an *intention profonde* that both defines and calls us.

The trying California period also gave me some academic gifts to bring back to Emory. A psychology professor had started a course on death and dying at Sacramento State in the early seventies. He was impelled in this direction by the illness and death of his wife. I sat in on his course from time to time with the psychological death of my first marriage hovering over my shoulder. At Emory I started a death and dying course that became popular. Issues of physical and psychological dying were, after all, central to all religious traditions. After psychiatrist Elisabeth Kübler-Ross's pathbreaking book on the dying process, the medical establishment opened up to new ways of thinking about the end of life. The hospice movement gained ground, and death counselors like Buddhists Stephen Levine and Ram Dass engaged in new styles of pastoral counseling among AIDS patients and others on the final journey. It was always a high point in the course to have an AIDS patient and nurses who took care of him address the students. Privileged college students usually hadn't seen death at close quarters. Student journals reflected seldom asked questions about life choices in terms personal mortality.

Just as the topic of death and dying focused on deep challenges to the psyche, my sessions with David Garrett drew me further into psycho-spirituality. The more I studied Jung outside of our therapy sessions, the more I saw religious myth and ritual as dealing less with stuff out there, as it were, and more with issues of conscious an unconscious life such as matters of personal becoming. Yet I wanted to balance this inward momentum. My interests in peace studies during this period kept me aware of the social ramifications of religious traditions. Moreover, the waning days of the Vietnam War made it virtually impossible to ignore politics. But even more, my own pain, intensified by an unwanted mid-life divorce, affected my mind and heart. For me the battleground at this time remained mainly inward. I have always tended to develop new courses at Emory in keeping with my own enthusiasms. So I started a graduate seminar on Jungian psychology and religion. Jung's writings were an attempt to translate the seeming externalities of Christian myth into a language of psychic development. Where Freud brought the gods back down to earth to eliminate them in the light of science, Jung grounded them as important elements in our psycho-spiritual journey. My later explorations of Buddhism and Taoism would fit in well with such interests. Eastern traditions honor the contemplative aspects of the human psyche.

In keeping with this psychological turn, driven by my own experiences, I initiated another graduate course on autobiography and spirituality. Here a considerable body of literature already existed from Augustine's *Confessions* to contemporary works by Thomas Merton and Dorothy Day. Moreover, the wider realm of novels and memoirs provided a rich source of autobiographical reflection. But it was my life story newly revisited by the shock of divorce that motivated me to start this course. (And forty years later, here I am doing self-story yet again.) The psychological turn in my life also influenced how I taught other courses with undergraduates. In a course on dreams and religion, students kept journals of dream reflections related to their past and present histories. They began to see the world of dreams as symbols for exploring their own usually ignored emotions and life histories. In a college milieu of much extroversion, I was inviting them to walk a more introspective path. They also sketched their dreams in color once they got over the fear of not being able to draw.

Although never a strong social activist compared to others from religious communities, I've been an intellectual liberal on many issues. Some Jesuits, for example, have devoted themselves intensely to liberation theologies that impelled them to live with the poor and marginalized. Protestant colleagues in Atlanta, propelled by their gospel vision, gave up on academic careers to open a community house for street people in the spirit of the Catholic Worker movement. My level of involvement in this venture was to become the Grits Man at Sunday morning breakfasts where I ladled out this southern favorite to lines of homeless people. And I would make financial contributions to such causes. In recent years, I've become a chastened liberal aware of the limits of producing the blessed community through social engineering. While I admire peace and justice movements in religious communities, I fault them for their frequently simplistic critique of "neo-liberalism." Religious critics of capitalism often confine themselves to moral generalities about justice. But they fail to do their homework on how complex economic systems actually work.

All this is prelude to why I was not satisfied to focus only on courses dealing with our inner lives. My second book, *The Religious Experience of Revolutionaries*, and my subsequent sabbatical in Berkeley exploring human violence, indicate my interest in social problems. On returning to the university, I attempted to start an interdisciplinary program in peace studies. A number of colleagues contributed to the proposal, but it foundered in the curriculum committee. Interdisciplinary programs were relatively new at Emory. Academic fiefdoms jealously held their turfs. But I did teach a course on peace and violence in the Religion Dept. I then turned my efforts to organizing a national conference at Emory on a curriculum for a national peace academy. A movement to establish such an institution in Washington was already under way. I worked with the leaders of the national campaign for a peace academy to bring outstanding scholars from around the country to Emory for a conference in 1978. At that meeting I would meet my present wife,

Peggy Herrman, whose mentor in mediation studies, Jim Laue, invited her to facilitate some sessions. Peggy and I remember that we definitely "saw" each other for the first time at that gathering. Then she found out that I was married to "that good-looking red head."

My new courses and added involvement in graduate studies (I had become chair of the theology section) satisfied my intellectual life. But my social and emotional sphere was another matter. I was feeling the gap left by C's exit. Of course, I see this better in hindsight. Friends and advisers urged me to go slow before committing to another woman. On an intellectual level, I agreed completely with this advice, as I recorded many times in my journal. It was clear that I didn't know C well enough before marriage. I moved too quickly from the Jesuits to marrying her. All this made sense in my mind. but I was still dragging along old habits and longings as I met new women. The partially unspoken question was "Is this the one?" I hadn't reached the kind of spiritual maturity that would allow me to be at peace with my own solitude. In practice, I was far from cultivating the inner feminine, in a Jungian sense, that might slow me down in the pursuit of women.

If I ask why this was so, I would have to look into the always murky zones of my deepest fears and yearnings. It probably had to do with a primordial fear of abandonment or rejection that went back to early childhood. Was it in part the strong attachment to my mother and identification with her plight in the frightening world of my father's rage? A woman would be there to protect me then and now when these anxieties crept back. Was it my own underlying fear of death that is connected with being separated or cut off from the comforting other? (Here I think of Plato's myth of the human person as a circle that was cut in half and constantly longs to be reunited with the separated part.) Whatever the origin of my tendencies, my life during this time illustrates the power of emotion on our minds. In recent years, much has been written about the importance of our emotive intellect. As I describe the sagas of new dealings with women, I am talking about stages of spiritual development. The evolution of spirit in us unfolds in the painful and joyful steps we take in the specific events of our lives.

As my relationship with a California woman ended, I took up with a friend at Emory. She was a bright, tall blonde, some years my junior, a native Atlantan who had been at the college for a few years as an associate dean. We had a good deal in common and similar interests in higher education. Conversation was always easy whether about her past in the Head Start program or about her interest in the arts. She liked me, enjoyed doing things together, but she lacked that sensual spark toward me. Our sexual attempts were rather perfunctory, in large part because my old quick trigger problems had revisited. Yet in part this malfunctioning stemmed from her own hesitancy about the two of us as a permanent item. The old cliché of "It takes two to tango" was at work. Yet our lack of mutual passion may also have contributed to keeping alive a good friendship that would last many years.

As I review my journals, I see ingrained Jesuit patterns still at work. In the *Spiritual Exercises*, Ignatius has rules for coming to important decisions in life. The first might be called the overwhelming event that leaves little doubt about making the right choice: Paul struck blind on the road to Damascus. I doubt that I have the temperament for such decision-making. The gods don't visit my psyche with thunderbolts. With these between-marriage relationships, I had selected the second method, a rational analysis of the pros and cons of each woman listed in separate columns. I had many entries under each column. It would make an accountant proud. Here are a few examples: "secure but smokes and fears flying; intensity: moderate; body: attractive and could like sex; conventional Christian; earthiness undeveloped;" For another: "secure, doesn't smoke, can fly; intensity: high; body: attractive and likes sex strongly; engaged Christian; earthiness developed." After making the lists, I added that I couldn't really choose a woman in such a mathematical mode. I wasn't buying clothing from a rack. I had to show the woman that I appreciated her for herself. Ignatius offers a third and preferred mode of decision-making: listen closely for the consolations of the Spirit within one's own heart. But I was then too impulsive with women to allow those consolations to mature over time.

My Emory friend would eventually marry the Nobel poet, Czesław Miłosz, and enter a new world of writers and artists. I remember the night she brought Miłosz to read his work to a packed chapel. I walked in late and caught a glimpse of her profile in a kind of rapturous listening. At that moment, I sensed something more between them. Later on trips to their home in Berkeley, I enjoyed hospitality and lively conversation over good red wine. Czesław referred to me as "her Jesuit." I think he had doubts about my reformist ideas for the church. As a Polish intellectual who made his way to Paris in the 1920s, he was leery of all utopian schemes from right to left. I didn't think that democratizing the church was all that utopian, but I was dealing with the world-weariness of a European intellectual. I represented American idealism to him, the rather naïve élan of being able to reform human nature in its proclivities toward power and corruption. I was shocked to hear of my friend's early death. She is buried in the old Decatur Cemetery near Atlanta. I think of her often as I drive by her resting place.

My relationship with B is a strange story of collapse and renewal, of a tormented marriage and a strong lifelong friendship. From hindsight it looks like a kind of humane victory drawn from self-inflicted defeat on both of our parts. It brought out the best and the worst in us. The beginning was very good for me, but things went downhill quickly. B taught economics at Emory. One day in the fall of 1976 I leaned over to Will Beardslee, a mentor and colleague, in the faculty dining room and asked about the redhead at another table. Then by a strange coincidence a friend of B's called me to contact her because she was very down about the ending of a relationship. The friend probably thought I had some pastoral counseling ability, or maybe she was also match-making in an intuitive way.

The pastoral counseling never got started as I was intensely attract-ed to her. The sexual element was powerful for me (I think less so for her), but I also enjoyed her intelligence, excellent taste in life style, and I knew that she was a very honest person, the kind that wouldn't steal a dime. Moreover, she treated her parents and friends kindly. I didn't give myself enough time to see clearly the value clashes and the emotional "hot buttons" ready to be pushed under the surface of an exciting ro-mance. Or perhaps I was naïvely thinking that the red flags in the early months could be put to rest by two mature persons of good will. But in hindsight I know that I placed too much emphasis on the early glow of strong attraction without giving it time to play out.

We met in late September and were married in December, 1976. I suppose that in a more ideal world, a short courtship might work. But my journals announced loud and clear that such beatitude was not around the corner. Even before the wedding, my judgmental attitude came into play. B blew up when I criticized her for taking a drink before going to bed. I was operating on my fears of C's tendencies with alcohol, and B reacted to what she saw as paternalism and criticism of her good judgment. She was still stressed and very tired after her recent breakup.

And for the most part, she talked about her life at Emory in negative tones. She didn't really enjoy being an economist and resented pressures to publish. In a way, she stumbled into the "dismal science" through a respected college mentor and perhaps to please her father who would see this career path as practical and therefore worthy. Her best talents lay in working with people and in her gifts for the aesthetics of fashion and interior design. She saw anything that sounded like a psychological critique from me, especially if it touched on her family history, as a terrible put-down, a damning judgment about her.

She would upset me by a testy, critical tone of voice that began with "O, Gene." I had only to hear that intonation to feel both depreciated and angered. It could be about the way I started to dress for an event. (She did class up my act in things sartorial, however. I've told her later that she trained a somewhat seedy former Jesuit to look better in public.) It was the little things that put us on the rack. In my perseverating way, I would not hear how she wanted something done at a dinner party: "O, Gene." On a trip, I would choose places to stay that weren't upscale enough: "O, Gene." I objected to her buying (she had the good sense not to in the end) Tiffany place settings for $180 a piece: "O, Gene." I didn't give enough time and attention to her family or friends when they visited: "O, Gene." Married or just living together, people recognize these subtle voice modulations that bring on strong negative feelings and subsequent angry outbursts. Spiritual directors and therapists would see them as occasions for inner growth if handled wisely.

We did have different attitudes about material things. B loved beautiful fabrics, and she resented what she called "Penneys inventory rejects" that she received in childhood from her father, a J. C. Penneys store manager. Looking very good was important for her self-image. I wondered how much being a twin with a birthmark on her lip had played into her not recognizing her own very good looks. But again, we were back to the resented psychoanalyzing on my part: "O, Gene." My attitudes toward material things differed. I arrived on the scene in an old Dodge Dart with awful early seventies clothing. She saw that a major reconstruction was called for. But more importantly I carried with me a Depression era mentality that penury was just over the hill. The Jesuits built on that view with the vow of poverty. Luxury items seemed wrong to possess for a Christian looking at world poverty. Her response to my scruples was: "You won't help the poor by being poor." Our political ideas were reasonably close as we both rejoiced in Jimmy Carter's victory in 1976. A big boost for her came when she received an appointment to the Federal Impasse Panel where she worked as an arbitrator. Operating as a judge in labor disputes put her in direct contact with people. She would later develop a successful practice as a divorce mediator.

But our relationship kept seesawing downward within the first year of marriage. She didn't feel loved or emotionally supported. I was, in her mind, becoming her worst critic, and I was too wrapped up in my work to notice her needs. I saw that if I backed off without responding to a perceived accusation, we would not escalate into a bad scene. As part of the back and forth, she would say that she loved me or leave me a note with that message when we seemed at the brink of parting. I'm sure she did love me and still does. As a counter to my workaholic tendencies, I expressed in my journal a desire to meditate and return to a quiet inner place to assess what was going on. I thought it would be good for her, too, to explore the practice of contemplative spirituality. But in our troubled circumstances, such a suggestion from me would not have worked. She would have taken it as the antagonist criticizing her for not being religious enough. It would have added fuel to the fire. Later I wondered how many people could be helped in their marital problems not just by therapists, but also by contemplative teachers. I think we were meant to become not only psychologically smart but spiritually mature. Here the wisdom traditions have much to offer.

Yet the issue of religion presented another lacuna in our lives. Once she got to college, like many others of her generation, B had given up on the rote Irish-American Catholicism of her father. It was largely a religion of rules about going to church on Sunday, not eating meat on Friday, and avoiding certain sexual practices, all under threat of serious sin. The wider mystical traditions of Christianity were largely unavailable to the average Catholic. But it could also be that some people are "religiously unmusical" as Max Weber said of himself. I think he was talking about the usual language and ritual of religion, not about religions taken as wisdom traditions. B's religion expressed itself in her kindness to friends and in her highly sensitive ethical conduct. It was too bad that I didn't appreciate that kindness to others as the hallmark of real religion in her.

But in our everyday lives, we kept cycling between good moments of truce and frequent explosions. Before a year was out, we had talked about divorce, but neither of us wanted to take the step. This repeated marital brinkmanship led to B's losing interest in sex. The relationship was fast becoming a limbo, an arrangement. She felt attacked and on trial with "a fundamental lack of empathy" from me. I concluded that I wasn't the right man for her. I reacted badly to what I saw as her need to control, to use me as a lightening rod for expressing deeper frustrations about herself. I couldn't figure out how much of her reaction to me stemmed from my shortcomings as a husband (according to her image of this role) and how much of her dissatisfaction came from unresolved struggles within herself about self-image and workplace disappointments. But I realize that such statements can be a form of self-absolution on my part, getting me off the hook of self-reform. As much as I hated to face another divorce, for all of its public and private mayhem, I tried to unlatch inner spiritual resources to find the best path, accept the pain of my own limitations and move on.

While my teaching went well and I was enjoying new courses in dreams and death and dying, pressures from senior members of my department aggravated troubles at home. They decided that I wasn't ready to be put up for full professor. They saw my many publications, usually in article form, as the work of a good journalist or public intellectual. John Palms, the college dean, asked: "What is his field? He seems to move around every few years." They thought my work had declined since *The Religious Experience of Revolutionaries* (1972). It's hard to know how much the divorce and the newly agitated marriage fed into this perceived decline. They said that I needed to publish something of scholarly density, a serious book with solid methodology that opened new ground. I had nothing against my colleagues for saying this. They spoke with obvious concern for me. Martin Buss, a biblical scholar, said that he admired my many writings and other contributions. He himself didn't like writing for reward. Martin said that he would support me if I wanted to keep writing as an essayist, but I should not expect rewards from the university.

I asked myself both what I thought about all this and how I felt about it. The questions are related but are also distinct. I did see myself as an intellectual essayist, an interpreter of ideas and not a research scholar in the usual tradition of the university. In a minor way I was operating as a public intellectual, a term that would later come into wider usage. I saw the university as too narrow in what it considered good scholarship.

A few years later, in a major national study on the nature of scholarship and promotion in higher education, Ernest Boyer would corroborate my views. He argued that the university should have a valued place for publications that did not break new ground, but that interpreted scholarship for a wider audience. The university, he urged, should honor and reward a portion of such scholarship in its professorial ranks.

Yet the honest talk from my colleagues paid off in my research. In 1982 I published *Aging as a Spiritual Journey*, which reviewers saw as "a little classic" in the neglected field of aging. In that book, I put together the field work of interviewing religious elders with re-interpretation of religious teachings and psychological perspectives. I was then promoted to full professor. Writing about the spirituality of aging came as something of a surprise. I backed into it from my course on death and dying. As I looked around for good readings on the last phase of life, I realized that there wasn't much quality literature available. It was a largely unplowed field. So I picked up the plow.

But how did I feel about the judgment of my peers? Even though I half suspected this assessment from colleagues, I was more affected than I thought. I lost sleep over it. I was not beyond caring what others thought about me. My ego longed for approbation from important people. I was still a good distance from the reaction of an enlightened person who was truly detached from the outcomes of his actions. Such an outlook may be a good definition of a saint or bodhisattva. And yet my spiritual training in the Jesuits pushed me to ask important questions. What counted, what was of value for me as I approached fifty? In part, the answer formed itself in still another question: what valuable contributions could I make as a teacher, writer and person? But on a deeper level, I challenged myself with the perennial query: *Quid hoc ad aeternitatem*? ("How does this stack up against eternity?")

I didn't think in terms of rewards in an afterlife, but rather what spiritual meaning did this episode have for my life in the present. How could I make creative use of this unpleasant experience? We need outer encouragement, but as we mature, our inner guru should take over. I could hear the voice of Ignatius Loyola, with whom I would disagree on various points, calling us to put away the "honors and glories of the world" to embrace the paradoxes, the small deaths of life.

As I move back to the saga of marriage to B, I want to underscore the spiritual values above as linked to our difficult relationship. She was religiously unmusical to the chords I tried to play. Was it the limits of a very constricted, girlhood Catholicism of rules that never opened her up to the richer wisdom of Eastern and Western heritages? But one thing seemed clear: I might do better with a partner who could resonate with me on a spirit level. Yet this conclusion does not absolve me from looking hard at what I could learn from the trials of our marriage. Moreover, these deeply upsetting events were more than merely psychological stressors. They constituted real challenges along the spiritual path. It's unfortunate today that few appreciate such marital problems as invitations to inner religious growth.

Wise teachers tell us that we don't grow by merely thinking about spirit life or by imagining ourselves as enlightened persons or saints. A Buddha might say that it's all about practice in the imperfect reality of the here and now. Or to put it another way, our sessions with two therapists pushed me to examine some of the roots of my responses to B. In important ways, such psychologizing becomes a modern language for spirituality. It's ironic that we may learn more about ourselves from a bad relationship than from a good one. I was less able to deceive myself about my virtues. In a more realistic view, I saw myself excessively judgmental towards those closest to me and prone to quick anger. I began to grasp more clearly my fear of being alone and my tendency to be hard on myself through a life of striving to attain goals. I also understood that I cared too much about what others thought of me, not only academically but as an inadequate husband.

B and I became aware of deep-seated problems for a viable future together. On one level, our value priorities caused friction: different attitudes about money, material things, and common goals for the future. This could be summarized in her words: "we are pulling in opposite directions." Related to value issues were the daily disappointments for her that would lead to angry exchanges over minor events. I might have bungled how men should act in her eyes. Our sex life had largely come to a halt. In late November of 1977, I wrote in my journal: "Is there enough hope for the relationship? Can I continue to come home to an unhappy person who resents my unloving presence? Can I continue to put myself in a situation where I am seen as the cause of her grief? Will counseling help? I'm willing to try it. Still I wonder if we can ever change our basic feelings." In our novitiate Long Retreat, we learned about the purgative way on the spiritual path, a painful but cleansing awareness of our inner selves. Yet that was child's play compared to the purgative way in a troubled marriage. Here was the spiritual furnace in the specifics of life not in the artificial circumstances of formal religion.

As I prepared for our sessions with a pastoral counselor, I thought about what I found positive in B: her lively personality, her kindness to family and friends, her sense of honesty, her physical attractiveness. Yet I also I struggled with her demands for change in me: be present, be caring, be a friend, be on her side. It was as though with a modicum of effort, I could throw a switch and be all those things in the ways she would accept. I hoped we could in therapy get at some of the under-lying issues and turn things around. I wondered how much she might be transferring to me her anger about a dearth of affection from her father. On my side, the lack of early modeling of a good man-woman relationship and my emotional retardation from years in a religious or-der played into the marital crisis. But in our first session, the counselor noted something that I would surely have missed about myself. After I went through a litany of how I heard B's grievances and how I felt about them, he pointed out that I failed to reflect on my own affective needs. I had talked about changing to please the other. He opened a door for me that would later be further clarified when we worked with a sex thera-pist. Pleasing others for approval and security had a long history in my psyche from childhood to life in the Jesuits. Many of us curry favor with others without consulting our own needs.

Therapy helped us filter what we had been saying privately through a new listener. He could hear both our thoughts and emotions and pos-sibly put the sorry story into a new context. That gave us both a glimmer of hope that we were getting off dead center. But for me therapy had another effect. It gave me a new sense of how dire our marital situation was. The space provided by an experienced listener allowed me to step back, as it were, and by not reacting with the old patterns of defensive emotion, hear her pained expression in its fullness. If things are really this bad, I thought, there wasn't much hope for a better future between us. Underneath the usual complaints between us, the therapist helped us surface again the historical context of our getting together. She was rebounding from a failed relationship with all of its intense sexual and "masculine" expectations that I seemed unable to meet. And I was in my usual rush to overcome loneliness when our sexual relations, from my perspective, seemed to work well. It was a deadly asymmetry at that season in our lives. We both needed more time alone or at least outside of the close demands of marriage. The old adage summed it up: marry in haste, repent at leisure. In my impulsiveness, and driven by both of our compulsions to not be alone, I had failed to listen to advice from friends to *festina lente*, make haste slowly.

But even beyond the weak sand on which we stood when we married, the therapy sessions underscored seemingly irresolvable conflicts. There was her constant complaint about not feeling loved. She saw me as her critic and not her friend. We differed about spending money and how much material things could make us happy. Yet I was hardly the poor monk with begging bowl. During this period, I began to buy rental property and also get a real estate license. My involvements with peace groups and Amnesty International did not bother her. Nor were our views on politics (both Jimmy Carter Democrats) and economics (she had a tempered view of capitalism) all that different. The problems were in close: this Mercedes, that expensive hotel, that fur coat, that higher-end restaurant. Then I heard her drumbeat about my lack of masculinity, not in a physical sense as if I had effeminate qualities. Rather she saw me as a befuddled professor rather than the sort of worldly professional on whose arm she could feel like the loved princess.

Her put-downs would often bring explosive responses from me. She might then sleep downstairs or in another room. Anger coming back at her was something she had known neither from her family background, which suppressed negative emotion, nor from her first husband, a silent, repressed type. She interpreted my anger as not liking her for who she was. If I suggested that she might be happier with a different man, she would see that as a cop-out on my part, leaving open for her the greatest dread: being alone and abandoned. Beneath all the *Sturm und Drang*, lurked dual issues: her negative self-image and enough value differences between us. I decided to stop seeing the therapist earlier than she did. I wanted to let things settle in my mind and work toward a firm response to her. Eventually the counselor suggested separation or divorce as a solution. Again we were at the edge, but neither of us had the courage to take the step and face the consequences.

In a local restaurant, I half seriously suggested to B that I had left the vows of a religious order to take them up again with her. I joked that her spending orientation would keep me poor, her withdrawal from sex, celibate, and her demands to do things a certain way would keep me obedient. But problems with sexuality brought us to the final stage of our marriage. We know that sex isn't the most important aspect of a good marriage, but the tension caused by lack of it reveals underlying problems. We saw a woman sex therapist who explored the history and playing out of our anxieties that brought us to a sexual impasse.

She noted that I had learned from childhood to be anxious in the face of my father's unpredictable wrath. I compensated for it by intellectualizing, being aloof from emotional challenge, and by trying to please, especially my mother. I would try to be nice to keep the anxiety levels down, until pushed to the edge by B's pressing my buttons, and then I would explode like my father. She also pointed out that my quick anger at such moments curtailed empathetic listening. These deficits of empathy (I've heard about them from every woman in long relationships with me) may well have originated from my need in childhood to escape the bottomless pit of my mother's self-victimization, which demanded that her elder son be eternally empathetic toward her. My survival instincts told me that I couldn't do it. As a boy, I would run out of the house and play with friends. But now there was nowhere to run.

Being nice fit in well with the priesthood. That's what church folk expected and rewarded. With a kind of passive-receptive attitude in the order, I was in some ways transforming my mother's victim traits into holy obedience and self-sacrifice. My reformist rebelliousness in the church was similar in some ways to expressing my anger at Gino Natale and simultaneously imitating it. It wasn't so simple, of course, in my later Jesuit days. By then I had marshaled solid arguments against authoritarianism in the church. I saw myself as a reformer with causes. And I still think this is true in my work to democratize the Catholic Church in the spirit of Vatican II. But at a gut level, underneath the theological and historical reasoning, my reaction to the authoritarian hierarch is in part the boy's feeling toward Gino Natale as household dictator. A good contrast to my reaction would be that of a lifetime Jesuit friend Jim Torrens. I knew his father well enough to discern that at home he was the opposite of Gino Natale. I've often wondered how much of my friend's easier obedience to superiors was conditioned by a more benign relationship with his father.

The counselor was trying to help us move out of the limbo phase of unhappy cycling between moments of hope and hours of dissatisfaction. An unusual "ah-ha" event happened to me in early 1980, something that Jungians call synchronicity. It didn't become a decisive factor in the outcome of our marriage, but it was so unbidden and dramatic that it's worth mentioning. I was on my way to do interviews in North Carolina for my first book on the spirituality of aging. I had driven about five hours to a Holiday Inn in Waynesville with the sun receding behind the mountains above Maggie Valley. I was pondering our marital crisis most of the day. When I opened the motel door, the room was very dark with only a ray of sunlight shining on an open Gideon Bible. I thought of Augustine's *tolle, lege* (take up and read) experience. The text was open to Ezra 10:11 which reads "Now, therefore, make confession unto the Lord God of your fathers, and do his pleasure. And separate yourselves from the people of the land, and from strange wives." I thought of both C and B. We had become strangers to one another. The Bible imperative seemed to say: stop the indecisiveness and make a move. Shortly afterward, I bought a condominium as B and I agreed to a structured separation that led some months later to a divorce.

That we have been able to maintain a good friendship for the last thirty years surprises many people. The same is true toward her mother who remained a real second mother to me. I visited her frequently in Atlanta until her recent death at ninety-six. I have never been one to throw away my history whenever I could avoid doing so. I keep photo albums of years past and other memorabilia. Certainly my journals for half a century attest to the desire to keep bridges open. This tendency ties into my Myers-Briggs personality type, a feeling-intuitive. Such people filter present experiences through the prism of the past, attempting to link feelings then and now. My attitude towards the Jesuits reflects this penchant. I have made a point of visiting Jesuit friends over the years in California and elsewhere. Once the tensions of our troubled marriage faded, B and I found ourselves friends again. We have supported each other in various ways for many years. She was instrumental in bringing me to my present wife, Peggy. By writing a personal ad, I helped her find a physician who is her partner today. Human relations are ultimately mysterious. Our continuing friendship satisfies needs on both sides, just as it perplexes others. I tell people in jest that I should have been born a traditional Muslim with an option of four wives. But of course, I know better given the string of my deficiencies with the ladies. The casual or informal harem is about all I can handle. In reference to B, I tell my present wife, Peggy, that love is not a zero-sum game, meaning that we can love more than one woman. She smiles wryly.

Throughout this period, I tried to draw from different spiritual traditions. I've always been attracted to the Christian theme of the indwelling of the Holy Spirit. Pentecost was always my favorite festival of the liturgical year. Holy Spirit theology breaks through the narrower dictates of the church and places religion in a much wider perspective both within oneself and in the wider world. The Spirit blows where she will. Yet a clearer understanding of my psychological tendencies brought home to me how far I still was from the letting go of my conditioned desires and their outcomes, a letting go that would have given me more peace of mind. Adversity brought out my weaknesses, a step on the journey to enlightenment.

Early in my years at Emory, a group of student devotees introduced me to the Indian teacher, Meher Baba, who "left his body" in the late sixties. My student Charles Haynes, then president of Emory's student body, knew Baba in the fifties when he visited a retreat center at Myrtle Beach dedicated to his perspectives. My visits to the Baba Center made me aware of the broader reaches of the Spirit through a form of Indian spirituality. At the Baba Center one felt an almost tangible sense of kindly interaction among people in an atmosphere of reverential silence in a virtually untouched natural environment along the South Carolina coast. I thought B and I would have gained much if we both might incorporate some of the Baba attitude of mutual love. I could not become an uncritical devotee of Baba like his closest followers with their complete "bhakti yoga" devotion to him. But I thought that Baba and Jesus must have shared similar mystical union with the divine. Their charismatic presence drew disciples to them. Later I would think this to be true of the Dalai Lama, whom I was to meet at Emory.

These experiences, as well as wider readings in history of religions and in New Testament studies, changed my understanding of traditional Christology. I saw the divinizing of Jesus by the early church as an exaggeration, although understandable in its cultural context. With a revised grasp of the avatar teaching of Hinduism, I was coming to see these specially graced beings as guides to help us appreciate our own inner "divinization," to use an Eastern Orthodox term. I will return to this topic when I discuss how the Jesus Seminar influenced my thinking.

My grasp of a more universal world of spirit relates to what I was realizing in the ups and downs of marital challenge. Much of what I have written in this chapter could be interpreted as merely a psychological struggle between a man and a woman. But this is too restricted a view. It would continue the conventional split between religion and psychology, the spirit realm and our psychic life. Distinctions are helpful, but dichotomies are often not.

One's deepest spiritual life is embedded primarily in daily choices and struggles, and only secondarily in religious institutions. In other words, what seem to be only interpersonal issues of marriage and other daily matters of choice and action are the bedrock of inner life. Theological language and religious ritual take on meaning in the specificity of our lives with others. So a psychological phase of my life became a deeply spiritual time for me. I had to live in the moment to moment concreteness of things, not in the meta-language of religious thought. I was learning not to confuse the map (religious theory and ritual) with the territory (my day to day life of choosing and acting). The finger pointing to the moon was not the moon.

1986: A NOVELIST IN FLORENCE

7

Coming Down to More Rough Landings

Have courage for the great sorrows of life,
and patience for the small ones.
And when you have accomplished your daily task,
go to sleep in peace. God is awake.

—Victor Hugo

THE TRANSITION TO THIS chapter was especially hard. I needed some of the courage and patience that Hugo talks about in the epigraph, especially in close personal relations. But even more than those virtues, I needed to learn to laugh with and at myself. We professor types tend to take ourselves too seriously. Add to that the weight of my background in a religious order. I was almost condemned to overestimate the importance of my doings. Swimming, hiking, painting, and poetry have been ways for me to kick back and let go of some professional heaviness. Cultivating friends was another mode of stress reduction. Companion animals, my dogs and cats, contributed much to unwinding over the years.

An insight came to me as I sat on a bench in Cortona, Italy, watching the cats of that medieval town go about their business. I was writing a poem about Cortona seen through the eyes of its cats. It struck me that these felines showed an earth spirituality in their tasks of finding food, guarding territory, and sunning themselves on Garibaldi's cannon in the town's square. Just before sitting near the cats, I had visited three old churches high up the steep streets. One sanctuary, dedicated to the penitent St. Margaret, required serious cardio-vascular exercise to reach.

Then it hit me. I had spent the first forty years of my life immersed in sky spirituality, the "up religiousness" represented by heaven-reaching spires. This is heavy stuff that didn't weigh down on the cats of Cortona.

Before returning home from Tuscany, I visited the Jesuit church of the *Gesù* in Rome, a baroque masterpiece of sky religion with St. Ignatius floating up to heaven in the apex of the ceiling. As a scholar of religion, I know that typologies of up and down are terribly loose and try to cover too much. But there is enough explanatory value in them to throw light on my situation, and maybe that of others.

Here are three working characteristics of sky religion. (1) The God or gods are transcendent, above us, with enormous power over us and the cosmos. (2) Their earthly representatives are kings or other usually male hierarchs who possess unique power from God, and are chosen by the divinity to rule over us. Look high up in the dome of St. Peter's to the clearly inscribed "Thou art Peter and upon this rock . . ." Popes have used that line to assert their divinely established power. (3) For us to be in conformity with God and his hierarchs, we must hold certain beliefs that imply cerebral activity over against our lower instincts. Of course, there are many other traits of sky spirituality, but these three will do for now. Although I use Catholic examples, sky religiousness is prominent in other branches of Christianity, especially as one moves right on the evangelical spectrum. A literal interpretation of the Bible becomes the sacred talisman (the scriptural pope) for their hierarchs.

Anthropologists of religion have shown the dominance of sky religion from Mesopotamia to Egypt to China and beyond. This movement is linked with vertical structures in economics and politics resulting from ever larger human settlements fostered by domesticating crops and animals. If we push back to earlier stages of human development, a reasonable argument can be made that spirituality in hunter-gatherer societies, even with the presence of shamans who visited other worlds, was more earth-oriented and less vertical. The pre-historic caves of Altamira and Lascaux display the art of an earth spirituality. In sum, sky religions/philosophies place ultimate power and meaning in the transcendent. Primal or prehistoric earth religions acknowledge and respect the centrality and fecundity of earthly life. This translates into differing emphases on natural or supernatural perspectives.

What can this excursion into up and down religion have to do with my life in the 1980s? A great deal, I think. A good barometer of my downward trend in religion could be noticed in conversations about the divinity of Jesus in seminars at Emory and with two Jesuit friends. Walking leisurely through San Francisco's Golden Gate Park, I told them

that I no longer held orthodox views about the divinity of Christ. I saw
Jesus as a great Jewish teacher and exemplar. The setting for this disclo-
sure was striking. We were walking by the de Young Museum, which
housed a remarkable Asian art collection of buddhas and avatars. I explained that my views were closer to those of early Christian theologian
Arius. His teachings, which were held widely in early Christian communities, refused to equate Jesus with God or to see him as second person
of the Trinity.

Rowan Williams, now Archbishop of Canterbury, in his scholarly work, *Arius: Tradition and Heresy*, notes that the majority of early
Christians did not see themselves as trinitarians: "Arians thought of
themselves . . . as Catholics or more accurately as the very wide spectrum
of non-Nicene believers thought of themselves as mainstream believers."
In contrast to this, he speaks of the Catholic model under Constantine
as "a monolithic social unit with a policy of religious coercion." Without
going into the technicalities of early church beliefs, they portrayed a human Jesus not of the "essence" of God as described in trinitarian theology. I don't hold the complex Greek metaphysics of many Arian bishops
who place Jesus above the angels but below God as a kind of adopted
demigod. (See Richard E. Rubenstein, *When Jesus Became God*.) Yet I see
this movement as a repeated counterpoint in Christian tradition to iden-
tifying Jesus with God. To be a modern Arian means finding God in the
full humanity of Jesus without turning him into the "Son" of the Trinity.
But the Arian movements lost out to the Athanasians who declared Jesus
to be fully God and man at fourth-century councils. Emperors were
themselves seen as divine personages. It wasn't a long jump to include
Jesus in that category.

I could tell that my friends were saddened to learn of my defection
from high Christology. (The terms high and low Christology have come
to demarcate Jesus as fully divine [high] or human [low].) Ed Malatesta
had done his doctoral work on the Gospel of John, a forerunner of high
Christology. To them, I had slipped away from true doctrine. It showed
a loss of faith, a diminution of spiritual health. It wasn't enough to have
faith in God. The correct way, the straight or orthodox mode, was to
believe in Jesus as Second Person of the Blessed Trinity. (I don't want to
slow down here for a more extended discussion of the meaning of faith,
but it's an important theme to take up later.)

I was breaking a main link in the chain of sky religion. Without a divine Jesus, it would be harder to uphold a sacred view of the pope, the vicar of the Christ-God, who teaches from on high. A lower Christology tended to relativize the papacy, making it the result of cultural conditions. It wasn't enough to imitate in my fractured way the virtues of Yeshua bar Yosef (Jesus), the great Jewish seeker and sage. I said that I continued to be gripped by his vision of a domain of God, a lifestyle of shalom in the here and now, a present realm of love, peace and forgiveness. And I believe that Jesus was divine as we all are, only more so. But this wasn't enough. For them I had pulled out the key to the vault of Christendom.

It didn't do much good to tell my friends that Jesus remained a Jewish reformer all his life, and that he never became a Christian. His life inspired the Christian movement, but the latter evolved after his death. Neither Jim Torrens nor Ed Malatesta could be classified as very conservative Christians. They were highly educated Jesuits open to ecumenical thinking after Vatican II. But neither of them saw the inconsistency of high Christology (the Christ before whom every knee shall bend in the introductory prayer for Mass on the feast of St. Ignatius after Paul in Galatians) and the new openness to Asian religions, for example. To make every knee bend in heaven and earth at the name of Jesus would we need new *conquistadores*?

As I write this chapter, I am reading a collection of poetry by Jim Torrens as a tribute to Ed Malatesta who died in 2002. When Jim's poetry turns to explicitly religious topics, he expresses traditional understandings of Jesus and Mary as crucial to the redemption of the whole cosmos. These are huge claims that I can't imagine Yeshua bar Yosef making in his lifetime. Ed devoted his last three decades to the old China mission of the California Jesuits. He wasn't trying to convert the Chinese to Catholicism in the mode of Jesuits from the time of Francis Xavier to the pre-Vatican II missionaries I knew as a young man. It should not be surprising that older Jesuits, as well as their Protestant counterparts, steeped in a high Christology as well as Augustine's teaching of no salvation outside the church, would be driven to baptize as many Chinese as possible lest they lose their immortal souls. In this missionary outlook, the well-intentioned but benighted Asians could not be saved within their spiritual heritages, which today we see as extraordinarily rich and worthy.

Malatesta established the Ricci Institute at USF for the scholarly study of Jesuit relations in sixteenth- and seventeenth-century China. Matteo Ricci, an early Jesuit missionary, was clearly ahead of his time as he entered the imperial court by the sharing his scientific knowledge. He also developed a deep appreciation for Chinese culture and dressed as a Mandarin. It is hard to know how convinced he was about converting the Chinese. Another aspect of Malatesta's efforts in China was to bring about a reconciliation between Chinese Catholics in communion with Rome and the state-approved church. This very tricky work was fraught with controversy, and Ed experienced his share of criticism as he soldiered along in the unification task. But I would be surprised if he thought that Eastern spiritualities (non-Christian, that is) were adequate in themselves to saving people. Otherwise, why the great effort to establish a native church in China? Wasn't it enough to share spiritualities with Asians, as if no one had the final answers claimed by sky religions?

My journey toward an earth-oriented spirituality had specific consequences in the early 1980s. It influenced my deliberations about becoming an Episcopal priest, and it affected my outlook on one day returning to the Roman Catholic priesthood. I had begun to explore the possibility of entering the Episcopal clergy. I recall conversations at Emory with Ted Hackett, an Episcopal priest-scholar at the Candler School of Theology. Episcopalians had a married priesthood and they also preserved the sacramental tradition. Sacraments maintain a "down" religion emphasis in their nature-oriented earthiness. And like the Roman Church, Episcopalians cherished a long wisdom tradition, not only of the Bible, but also of the succeeding centuries of saints and scholars. One reason for not going ahead with this option was a desire to continue working for reform within the Catholic Church where I had already established a public presence. I've always been able to distinguish between the many faults of my church and the best of its tradition. Some of this appreciation came from respect for scholarship and other aspects of my Jesuit heritage. It also arose from the charity and wisdom displayed by many Catholic people.

But as my Christology became lower, I could not in good conscience become a priest in either the Episcopal or Catholic traditions. The liturgy became the central stumbling block for me. Its core is based on a high Christology in which Jesus is the true God, the Second Person of the Blessed Trinity, who comes down from heaven to atone for our sins, and who then returns to his place as God's Only Son. This grand mythology or master story is still central to official church liturgy. I occasionally participate in both Catholic and Episcopal communities. I stress "official" or "traditional" liturgies because the less formal rites of house-church groups don't emphasize high Christology. As an occasional participant in traditional liturgies, I can figuratively reinterpret sections with which I can't agree. I can omit saying part of the Nicene Creed. Ah, the terrible "cafeteria Catholic" strikes again, I can hear critics say. But I would respond that any intelligent Catholic today is virtually bound in conscience to pick and choose. We can't stomach everything that is served up on the hierarchical cafeteria belt. But as an official priest of the church, I would be continually leading the liturgy as its celebrant and spokesman. I could not present myself that way and still be honest with myself.

Some would say—surely many at the Vatican but also across a wide swath of conservative Christianity–that I am neither a Catholic nor a Christian. They would argue that one simply can't take my stance toward high Christology and remain within the Catholic community. I'll return to this subject when I try to shape a comprehensive vision of my outlook. I can say briefly why I think I can be a low Christology Catholic Christian. Here are a few summary reasons:

(1) The Jewish Jesus (Yeshua bar Yosef) wasn't interested in dogmatic litmus tests for his disciples. What counted was their willingness to be open to living in God's domain of shalom expressing its virtues of love, justice, and forgiveness in present circumstances and in an unbrokered relationship with "Abba" or Yahweh. Jesus, while respecting his tradition, urged people to go beyond institutional rules to focus on deeper issues of commitment. Time and again in the Gospels he is calling his fellow Hebrews to revive the inner spirit of their own tradition over against external decrees. He repeatedly got into trouble with authorities for doing this. Again, it seems strange that we have to remind people of the obvious fact that Jesus was not a Christian. The point is that his own Jewish heritage did not impose theological beliefs for membership as would the Christian church centuries later. Finally, the Jewish Jesus, the only one who lived in history, would not have attributed high Christology to himself (the Jesus of the earliest strata of the New Testament reflecting his own teachings in sayings and aphorisms). High Christology was developed in the early Christian church. Even in the fourth-century forms

of low Christology were more prominent than trinitarian Christology in most communities. So if low Christology, as it were, was good enough for Jesus, why should it not be good enough for me?

(2) Despite its two millennia history, Christianity is still in its infancy. It is a work in process. The very early tendencies in the church as reflected in the New Testament toward seeing Jesus as God were partially conditioned by cultural imperatives and institution-building needs. An expanding hierarchy based its temporal and spiritual power on widespread acceptance of such divinizing tenets. Important rulers of the period invoked the gods to bolster their reign over people. It would be many centuries before the "divine right of kings" would give way to democratic governance. The church has argued that the Holy Spirit was particularly present in the formative Christian centuries, fixing monarchical hierarchies for all time. Such structures become the will of God, not to be tampered with except by heretics. It was very convenient for church power to turn God into a monarchist or an unchangeable lover of absolute monarchies.

It was also easier in a pre-scientific era to convince people of these teachings handed down by often self-serving authorities ("self-serving" does not mean bad or even hypocritical; they were just doing what came naturally in the circumstances). With the rise of scientific approaches in history and other disciplines, we are better able to understand the cultural contexts that shaped older belief systems. For the most part, the churches have yet to take seriously the impact of science and evolution on seemingly unchangeable core teachings. In the great sweep of human evolution, religions may still be in early stages of development. How will Christianity look two thousand years hence when the church is a bit more mature?

Moreover, many Christians, without explicitly reflecting on it, are today neo-Arians regarding Jesus. The view of Jesus as a great spiritual teacher and exemplar of virtue has had many adherents in history. Isaac Newton had to hide his Arianism so as not to lose his chance to be promoted to the Lucasian professorship at Cambridge University. Thomas Jefferson and other Enlightenment thinkers formed a vanguard of such thinkers. The Unitarian-Universalist Church provides another example of a movement that separated from traditional Calvinism's high Christology in eighteenth-century America.

In keeping with this downward movement in my thinking on religion, let me return to my marital experiences in the 1980s. I like doing the intellectual work of a theologian. But my concrete mind-emotion engagements in daily life give a fuller picture. It's relatively easy to look good as an intellectual, but less so as husband and lover. *Per aspera ad astra* ("from the tough experiences to the stars"). Some theologians don't have to take that route. They go from bright conceptual star to star. I know this temptation first hand. As a priest, I could sympathize with the troubles of others, but I avoided the *aspera* in my daily life, because no one challenged me at an emotional level. As a college professor, I could retreat into library research or see myself as the wise one in the classroom. If I talked about my spirit life in those contexts, it would take on abstract or academic language.

But the *aspera* of life pulled me down to pragmatics in my next married relationship. I'm not saying that everyone must go through the wringer of three failed marriages to grow in spirit. For others the *aspera* will consist of illness, disappointments, rejections, and other sufferings. But without encountering such life shocks, we are tempted by platitudes. I realize now how little control my mind had over my emotions and rosy expectations in the early 1980s. My journals of the two years between B and V (my third wife) are a glossary of "go slow," "get to know these women," right down to my brother's admonition to live with them for a while before marriage. I was mentally convinced that I would not rush things.

I dated a few women after my separation from B, but my main interim experience was to rekindle an old friendship with my Emory friend who eventually married Czesław Miłosz. She was still interested and we had a good deal in common as academics in the same school. We genuinely liked each other. As I said earlier, she was attractive: tall, blond and a good conversation partner. I found her a bit aloof, which turned out to be a healthy trait given my recent emotional wounds. While I tended to be headstrong in imagining future scenarios of man and wife, she held back, imposing a more casual cadence on our encounters. I didn't like her smoking habit, but even that smoke screen between us was a wisely protective device, making me work harder to see through it to discover what she really wanted beyond my projections. She knew how to slow me down without turning me off. She had also developed a fear of flying, which she eventually overcame. Whatever the psychological mechanisms of that airplane anxiety, fear of flying in a figurative sense was a good counter-balance to my impulse to fly at jet speed into new entanglements. She, like the Greek hero, Antaeus, felt stronger with both feet on the ground. I was off balance, and too ready, like Daedalus, to fly into the marital bliss of my fantasies. While my intellectual life during this period was moving earthward, my emotional core was still sailing upward, lifted like a spiritual balloon, toward connubial bliss.

Moreover, my sexual performance problems, inherited from two traumatic marriages, continued. She was understanding, and believed that these issues would be resolved over time. But at age fifty-one I worried about my fading masculinity. Yet she discerned that we were not meant for each other as man and wife for reasons that transcended sexual performance. She could see that there wasn't enough mutuality and joy between us. We were both making due. I was leaning on her like a shell-shocked victim of a just ended marriage. We separated amicably and remained friends. As I write these lines, I see a front page obituary in the *New York Times* of her husband, Czesł aw Miłosz, the Nobel poet, who died at ninety-three. Her holding off from marriage with me projected her into an extraordinary relationship with the Miłosz. My stays at their house in the Berkeley hills when they were traveling introduced me to Czesław's library and his long expatriate career through the turbulence of two world wars. But it also impressed me with the unbidden in life, or what Jung would call synchronicity: that Miłosz's poetry reading at Emory would help him find a second wife in my former girlfriend, a quiet person from Decatur, Georgia.

I now understand a couple of things about myself that I hadn't figured out well enough during that time. Chalk it up to hindsight. First, my emotions outrun my mind. My present wife talks about it as my being somewhat mercurial. Many recent studies reveal that all our mentation is emotionally conditioned. We are emotional minds. As I said, my journals offer many cautions against haste from friendly advice to self-exhortation about letting relationships develop gradually. I didn't want to repeat the misery of an alienated marriage nor did I want to look ridiculous in family and social circles. Movie stars could get away with this sort of thing, but not religion scholars. Yet despite all these signals, I was to founder a third time.

Another insight might provide a fuller explanation for my emotional drivenness. I had not made peace with being okay alone. Even though I longed for a more contemplative life, ironically I feared solitude. The goal of fostering a meditative inner life keeps recurring in my journals. Whether I was alone in a cabin in north Georgia with my standard poodle, Jenny, or on a retreat at the Meyer Baba Center in South Carolina, I was convinced that the best religious path for me was meditative or mystical.

Yet I didn't follow up on these yearnings with consistent spiritual practice that might have supplied more peace in my aloneness. All wisdom teachers talk about regular practices of meditation and other disciplines. I was filling up my alone time with the exploits of scholar, teacher, writer, and occasional lecturer. And I was running away from the uncertainties of solitude by seeking women who would shore me up emotionally. I had no problem with solitariness when scholarship and research required it. But my fear of being alone on an affective level created a complex of fears: abandonment, rejection, and ultimately a fear of death, that final letting go into our aloneness.

During the two years between B and V, I returned to therapy, motivated largely by concerns about sexual performance. My mind stayed in the zone of the earthy: a mid-life penis anxiety with some penis envy of those whom I imagined blessed with grand erectile talents. It was one thing to say that it was all in my head, that things would get better with a secure relationship. But if the brain-penis connection falters, especially in an era of high performance expectations, each new dating sequence resembles a pass-fail exam. I began to see a hypnotherapist. Maybe self-hypnosis, I thought, could help me relax and stop programming myself for failure. The therapist thought that anxieties from many sources undermined sexual coordination. He noted the burdens of family history, the long spell of celibacy in my formative years, and the collapse of two marriages. He taught me modes of self-hypnosis that might de-sensitize the old triggers for dysfunction. And we discussed the difficult question: did I unconsciously choose women who might victimize me? That query contains a huge overstatement, and it could let me blame women for my problems. But experiences with my mother from childhood may have paved the way for me to identify with her own self-victimizing. The therapist advised me to delay having sex with new women to avoid self-defeating experiences.

I met V in March of 1982 at a Presbyterian church-sponsored singles event. I found a tall, good-looking brunette with an enigmatic, enticing quality about her. Our first meeting shared in some of this hidden aspect. I had put an ad in a singles magazine. She responded by inviting me to the church singles party that she helped organize. But she didn't give me her name, only a general description. "If it's meant to be, we'll meet," she wrote. I actually met her in the crowd that night, but she didn't let on for a couple of days. Was she giving herself space to escape? Was she checking my pedigree? Did I look like a good bet only on paper? But when her phone call came, all banners were flying. The early weeks were intoxicating as I got to know her and her nine-year-old son. She was both reassuring and intense. The go-slow voices faded, as did my brother's advice: "a marriage will be as good as its courtship," and to live with her for some time before making it legal. But my weaknesses overcame prudence. Sad to relate, we were driving around looking at houses about a month after we met, and we decided to marry a month after that.

Later a therapist would tell me that I ignored the alarm signals of her three previous marriages. As my father might have said: "Dey see you (the sucker) comin." I get a chuckle now from his typical rejoinder, but I have no reason to doubt her honest hopes for a good marriage. All of us follow mixed motives in major decision-making. Some of these reasons are only partially conscious. From my side, she was very intelligent (a member of Mensa), a devoted mother, and she seemed warm and caring toward me. She was probably attracted by the security of a tenured college teacher and a move up for her son who could be in line for better schools. I don't believe that she wanted to marry me only for those considerations, especially after the pain of her failed marriages. But two wounded histories were on a collision course. We married on July 31, 1982, the feast of Ignatius Loyola, an ironic twist of sorts. Was this the self-induced revenge of my novice master who warned us about "white caps"? V wasn't a nurse and she didn't wear white caps, but in a maritime sense, white caps predicted a rough sea ahead.

A month and a half after the wedding, I was complaining in my journal about V's withdrawn and sad moods. She seemed distant and depressed. I felt that she was emotionally absent from me, as she threw herself into child-rearing and taking courses at Georgia State University to complete her teaching credential. She would say that I misjudged her gloominess for rejection. According to her, these apparent moods were only pensiveness. Moreover, she was afraid of being too happy in a relationship, she said, because of the devastating experience of a former husband leaving her for another woman. She feared letting herself be hurt again. She also noted that she was in a shattered state of mind after her son's father left, when she allowed herself to get into a brief marriage with an airline pilot who made her feel worthless and controlled like a child.

I wondered, without saying it, whether she had been abused earlier in life, and was playing out the victim in successive relationships. I knew her dad only in his later years when he suffered from dementia. Her mother was a classic recluse, a trait V replicated in our marriage by pulling away from me physically and emotionally. During a festive event, like one of my book signings, she would recede into a corner more or less alone. But given my history as a son of a supremely self-victimizing mother, I would have had to combine both genius and sanctity not to overreact to yet another woman victim at close range. I think V was telling me the truth about her damage and pain, but I was still Katie's boy.

Just as V's high IQ ratings couldn't assuage her sorrow, my intellectual accomplishments didn't quiet the fury from my childhood. I don't mean to absolve myself for negative reactions to V by blaming my mother. As an adult, I was responsible for my actions. Therapy can help one see this and move beyond the past. But old scripts had sunk in over my first two decades. We can alter such negative reactions, but not easily. Moreover, I was probably attracted to V for the very reasons that I was reacting badly to her syndrome of gloom. She became a replica of my mother as sad victim.

Communication problems underlie all unhappy marriages. Yet underneath this truism resides the vexing issue of mutual perceptions. Even when we try to grasp the intimate other for what she really is, our projections, formed from past experience, skew our understanding. I saw her as aloof from me and increasingly cool to a life of close affection. I frequently wondered whether she got into this marriage for ulterior motives. I provided a stable environment for her to go back to school for her teacher's credential. Also her son, soon to be a teenager, might benefit by having a man around. I put these thoughts aside in better moments between us. Surely, I would tell myself, she is in this for more than security and child-rearing. V saw me as misjudging her pensiveness for distance and lack of interest. She viewed me as domineering, interrupting her speech and treating her like a child.

In this context, it didn't take much to raise the decibels of bad feelings. For example, according to V, I was not treating her son as well as she wished. Occasionally I would lose my temper with him, and I claimed to be too busy with work to attend some of his sport and school events. She was partly right. I wasn't an adequate parent. I had little experience with children and I tended to get wrapped up in my own designs. Yet in various ways, she monopolized the boy, allowing me to touch his life only peripherally. But on the whole, I thought that he and I developed a reasonable *modus vivendi* for the five years of the marriage. My purchase of a partial ownership in a north Georgia mountain cabin provided another irritant. In 1979 I got a real estate license, after purchasing a couple of rental properties in the Emory area. My first sale was this mountain house to an ex-Jesuit friend, Tom Till and his wife, Gerri. In the early 1980s, Tom left Atlanta to take a teaching post at St. Andrew's College in North Carolina. Buying into the cabin made sense, as it gave us an occasional retreat at reasonable cost. I also rented the house to other Emory personnel on weekends. But V didn't like the place. She wanted me to buy a more expensive house in the same subdivision. That I went ahead with the purchase of the Till property (with my own money) further alienated her. She saw this as disregarding her views and not trusting her as a valued partner. In hindsight it probably was not a wise thing to do for marital bliss.

But I doubt that this episode, which gradually blew over, would have made much difference in our ill-starred union. The wider breakdown of emotional communication led to a recurrence of my old sexual dysfunctions. The factors for sexual malaise became overwhelming. Now it was no longer nervousness with a new woman. She showed no interest in sex with me. When the topic came up explicitly, she placed the burden of our sexual collapse on problems that I brought to the marriage. She never spoke about her own negative baggage concerning sex inherited from her own family background and failed marriages. I could only speculate on what hurts from her childhood and subsequent events she might be bringing to our sexual encounters. But I would probably be wide of the mark, since she didn't reveal this part of her past. Yet I feel fairly sure that in addition to our immediate problems, some older demons were at work in her.

I would try to put our difficulties in a wider perspective. V was an attractive and intelligent person, as well as dedicated mother and a hard worker in our real estate investments. I tried to build on some of the good moments between us. Often enough these happened after major fallings-out, when the specter of separation and divorce loomed. Neither of us wanted to go down that road again. And she was under many pressures: finishing her degree at Georgia State, changing jobs, her father's mental and physical decline, and the sudden death of a sister in an auto accident. She would say that she loved me and that we could work things out. She wanted us to restore our relation by doing small, enjoyable things together like going out for ice cream or helping her son build a toy car.

She noted that I was growing distant from them in the strange alchemy of mutual animosity. We decided to see therapists separately at first with the possibility of consulting them together as things progressed. I had a session with a psychic who said something that cut through much of the mental churning about the marriage. She told me to be gentle with myself, and that such self-oriented benevolence would spill over into understanding my wider situation. That's a hard message to hear after a half century of whipping myself to succeed on all fronts. The psychic could feel my self-severity, and was reminding me that the great wisdom traditions urged us to love ourselves as God loved us. It was like a white dove landing on my shoulder to startle me with a long buried insight. Yet the bird doesn't stay very long. The pressure of self-wounding habits sweeps back in.

I began to see another therapist who, in hindsight, was more Dr. Phil's tough love than Carl Rogers's kindly listening. Yet his forthrightness drove me to say both yes and no to him. He said that I lacked the ability to express my power with women. I had assumed a victim role with C, B, and now V. I was playing out my mother's victim style. Instead of being forceful with women from the start, he said, I would turn explosive at certain points. But I was too compliant, too much the suffering servant of Isaiah rather than the bold, assertive King David. The therapist was drawing from his Jewish background as he likened himself to David regarding women. He also noted that in sex I did not cultivate the spontaneous child in myself. In a session with both of us, V agreed with him. She missed those qualities in me that she had previously experienced with others.

But she refused to do therapeutic sex exercises to help me regain some confidence. She found it mechanical and repulsive, and she doubted that it did anybody any good. It's interesting in situations like this that each partner thinks the other does not enjoy oral sex. But in my view, V had a fairly rigid template about sex. It was to be spontaneous and passionate, almost always in the missionary position and problem free. Short of that, it became burdensome. The therapist saw that we were not ready for the exercises, that our pre-sexual encounters undermined the feelings that prepare for enjoyable sexuality. He was partly right, I thought, that our main problem was not sex but power and how it was distributed or denied between us.

He tried to be hopeful with us. He urged us to exchange intimacies short of full sexual encounter to avoid situations of failure and disappointment. But honest intimacy can't be programmed when good daily communication collapses. A repeated gesture offers the clearest symbol of the marriage. She would wear a sweat suit to bed and turn away from me. When asked by the therapist if she contributed to our sexual impasse, she replied: "My problem is being in circumstances with a person who has a problem." I thought about settling for a companionate marriage, but I didn't think it would work for either of us. Resentments would fester just below the surface and we would both feel deprived. The therapist's main theme was that I allowed myself to be emasculated by women, robbed of my masculine power. C did it by pursuing outside relationships. B did it by demanding that I conform to her image of the take-charge man of the world, and now V was doing it by her own control mechanisms of avoidance. Weekend after weekend she would go off to breakfast alone, saying that she needed space.

How and where do I feel potent? I would ask myself. In just about every other life involvement, I answered. In teaching, directing students, writing books and articles, running the graduate theological studies program, starting a national movement of former priests, beginning a real estate career on the side, and, especially, in my long and much cherished friendships. The therapist was partly right in pointing to my relinquishing of power with women. But I thought his analysis and solutions were too simple. "Power" is a loaded word with many meanings. Although he didn't mean using it coercively, his idea of power came down to a forceful masculinity in a conventional sense. It was still a kind of push power rather than the subtle power of attraction from the other's soul. The woman psychic hit closer to mark when she counseled me to be gentle with myself. The kind of power that works in a relationship is one arising from kindness and respect on both sides. But partners need to be at ease enough with each other to let that inner power surge. We need to rewrite old scripts on both sides. Good sex becomes a byproduct of this change. V and I couldn't get beyond our mutual blockages.

A colleague at Emory put me in touch with another therapist who took a different tack toward our problems. Where the former counselor stressed lack of manly power in relations with women, the new counselor emphasized my need to be more empathetic. He was building on my early history of family interchanges that lacked affection and stimulated patterns of victim-victimizer. Instead of empathetic listening, I learned to curb resentments until they expanded into defensive anger that poisoned things. He saw power problems as secondary to the lack of affective communication: listening for words and feelings from the other and not responding with sullen withdrawal or explosive outbreaks. The latter led to "de-potentiating" both myself and my partner. Affirming this in theory, of course, was one thing, putting it into practice after a five year decline in the marriage was quite another. A Rorschach ink blot test at the start of therapy underscored some of the origins of my ambivalence about affective responses. I saw two little girls entering a room with a table lamp lit and gifts arranged on the floor. As the children approached the presents, the lamp turned into the stern face of a woman with an Elizabethan hairdo and high collar who tells them to leave. The girls rushed out of the room in fear.

This tableau helped me to see more clearly my dual relationship with Katie. She was both a source of unconditional love but also of conditioned love driven by her own needs. She encroached on us in various ways. We became the overburdened objects of her affection and we were the sons who never measured up to her extravagant expectations. She showed plenty of love for us, but there was also a distance from us as we grew out of childhood. She was probably reflecting lack of affection from her own past and from her relation with Gino. She also controlled her feelings with conventional mental inhibitions, a habit that I inherited.

The new therapist pointed out how I intellectualize things away rather than let them touch my feelings. I functioned pretty well with people in the work world, but I also keep them at a distance, as a few friends have told me. I distanced myself by using Gino's anger in close relationships. With more education, I am better than Katie at intellectually breaking lines of affection. I also carried forward the sadness and anger of those early years, when I tried to negotiate parental tensions. All this old baggage mingled with my wives' own checkered histories. It gave us less hope for a long, affectionate relationship. I very much wanted affection from these women, yet I didn't show it to them in ways that would elicit the trust underlying affection.

The therapist tried to teach me affective listening and responding. He asked me to reflect on times when I experienced affection between or from my parents, especially after childhood. I remember coming home at lunchtime from parochial grammar school to find an upbeat mother with a specially prepared meal. But there was less of this kind of presence as I grew older. Of course, a male relates differently to his mother as he comes of age. But Katie's affection deficit arose in part from her own background. My grandmother was not emotionally demonstrative. She grew up in a world where harsh realities of everyday survival dominated other considerations. I saw virtually no expressions of affection between Katie and Gino.

I looked at old snapshots of family outings to Mosswood Park in Oakland. The weather and scenery were pleasant, but I could see the virtual truce flags that my brother and I were carrying. Katie could let down and laugh more spontaneously with a couple of women friends in the neighborhood, but even there most of the talk was about who was sick, whose husband was mean and drank too much. Katie lacked close peer friendships. Even her neighbor, Margie Isola, was more a sounding board than friend, because most conversations would circle back to Katie's own sad situation. She was caught in a kind of narcissistic spiral, enveloped in her unresolved psychic drama.

Toward the end of my parents' lives, I was looking for ways of affective rapport with them. Gino was seriously limited in movement and speech by a series of strokes. He sat on a green plastic kitchen chair with tubular metal legs. Occasionally he would reach out toward me and say with quiet sincerity: "Eugene, I wish you all good, that's all . . ." I sensed an affect in his tone and a gentler look that was missing in all the angry years. And he would refer to *tu ma* ("your mother") as she sat, sad and emaciated, in another kitchen chair. As he said it, he had a twinkle in his eye and a note of care in his voice. But it was too late for her to respond in kind after a lifetime of live-in separation. I never saw my father and mother kiss each other at home or in public. Yet her final words to me in the hospital, "Eugene, don't get nervous . . ." were, in her own tortured way, a turning beyond her sufferings to wish my happiness. I thought of Julian of Norwich's "and all shall be well" in my mother's final testament.

The most consistent affective presence in my earlier years was Uncle John, *Barba Gianni*. He would make me laugh by impersonating my father, "Lucca," as he called him. His humor took some of the sting out of the fights going on across the street. He referred to Gino as "*Marciume*," which means something rotten in Italian, because he heard my father say "*Questo è marciume*" ("This is rotten") as he was appraising some object. *Barba Gianni* also nicknamed Gino, *Marce,* (pronounced "march") as in: "How's *Marce* doing today?" He wasn't saying that my father was rotten. It was just the odd sound of the word that caught his fancy. For all his nervous breakdowns and other shortcomings, *Barba Gianni* became the village jester whose playfulness leveled pretensions.

The therapist attempted to save my third marriage by getting us to communicate beyond defensiveness, head talk, and animosity. While I still hoped for reconciliation, V thought our prospects futile. My therapy sessions made her take a hard look at five years of dissatisfaction. She also worried about raising her son on a diminished income should we divorce. Yet she could see how little we had in common. And she didn't think we could restore a mutually satisfying sex life. She began to say things like: "We aren't getting any younger, and this is no fun for either of us," as she went off for still another loner weekend. (I wondered if she might be seeing someone on these Saturdays, but I had no evidence of it, nor did I pursue it.) Moreover, it wasn't good for her son to live in a tense home.

I thought we could take more time together with the therapist, but we had actually turned a final corner, even though we didn't want to recognize it. I would vacillate, wondering if we were just letting ourselves be dragged downward by negative moods that became a self-fulfilling prophesy. I hated the stigma of a third divorce. The therapist could see that my main emotion was not sadness, but fear of facing the world as a three-time loser. Good friends advised me to hang on through the rough times in hopes of a better tomorrow. But they were outsiders not privy to the scale of the internal problems.

The therapist said that I gravitated toward women like V because they were familiar to me. In various ways, they replayed my relationship with Katie. He wanted me to break that choice pattern. V seemed to confirm his insight when she said: "I can't be the kind of person you need for closeness, and you can't be the kind that I need." The therapist surprised me with a remark that may or may not have applied to V: some people have a gut level aversion to intimacy after the early romance period. I thought about her loner and reclusive habits. (As the marriage was collapsing in 1987, I wrote a journal entry about criteria for a soul mate: spiritual/religious seeking; academic and/or humanistic interests; a long friendship with sharing at all levels; open to being surprised by grace over against my well laid plans." When I came across the entry years later, I penned into the margin: "Peggy.")

My brother also urged me to consult my deepest feelings and make a decision. Shortly before the end of the marriage, I sat in his well-used kitchen (he's a very good Italian cook) in the Oakland hills listening to his unambiguous counsel. He spoke forcefully: do I want to face more years of a loveless marriage? But his main message was more positive: figure out what makes you happy, what will give you peace in the remaining decades of your life. He told me not to worry about what others think. "Do they pay your bills?" he asked.

V surprised me by announcing that she had found a house to buy for her son and herself. We were able to settle financially in an amicable way, and soon I was living alone in my house on Castle Falls Drive about a mile from Emory. The therapist was a bit disappointed that I had not made the decisive move to end the marriage. Yet as I sat on my deck watching yellowed leaves fall from trees, I wrote about a new phase opening up for me. I felt that a heavy weight had been lifted: "I will want the company of women, but I need to resist that, too. Don't search for a wife but for a soul mate. Maybe for the first time in my life I can learn to be happy alone." I had finally learned not to rush into marriage.

Margaret (Peggy) Herrman, my present wife, came into my life for the first time in 1978 at Emory when she assisted with a conference on a National Peace Academy. I was married to B at the time, but Peggy and I felt a mutual attraction. "I thought you had cute "buns," and you looked like a sad monk with a cowl over his head in a recurrent dream of mine," she later said. I had lunch with her in 1981, but she was involved with someone else at the time. In late 1989, the fourth criterion above for seeking a soul mate, that of surprise, came into play. B, who had worked with Peggy in conflict resolution, suggested that I call her since we would have things in common. I remembered her as a bit formidable and intellectual. B assured me that she had a warmer side.

In late 1989 Peggy was giving a talk on mediation in B's class at Emory. She asked Peggy if she would like a call from me. When I phoned her for lunch, she said okay, but not for three weeks or so. I felt that the judges were holding up signs of four or five on that dive. How interested could she be if she puts off the lunch for a month? But it turned out otherwise.

If my twenty years in the Jesuits represented a kind of sky religion, the following two decades with largely unsatisfactory marriages brought me down to earth. I could no longer gloss over my mistakes of judgment and, especially, my emotional history with its shortcomings. I wonder sometimes how different it might have been if I had met and married Peggy before the other three. Such hypothetical musings don't get us very far precisely because they are not down-to-earth. The hand that was dealt me and that I partially dealt myself shapes my only experience. It brought confusion and stress as well as moments of love. It also taught me much about myself on a number of levels. I learned how my earliest family formation influenced my later choices and reactions. Yet beneath the exchanges with three wives, I got to know my deeper anxieties about aloneness and abandonment. Without experiencing this on an existential plane, it would have been much harder for me to grasp the dictum of Socrates, "Know thyself."

Perhaps the oddest venture for a scholar of religion was my avocation in real estate that started mainly in the late seventies and early eighties. Was I unconsciously imitating my grandparents in Oakland who invested in rental houses and apartments when loans for immigrants were difficult to obtain? Then one had to pay cash on the barrel head. I've often referred to my move in this direction as the expression of a perverse interest in both God and Mammon. Yet what could be more imbued with a spirit of earth? As every real estate agent knows, it's all about land and its "improvements." Real estate turned out to be an education about people and how they react when they're about to make the biggest purchase of their lives. The interplay between agent and client also becomes a school of frustration, diplomacy, midwifery, hope and sometimes despair. It all began in 1978 when I saw a for sale notice on an Emory bulletin board for a triplex. A graduate student of mine had put up the sign for her landlord. Was this a lure from God or Mammon? Not knowing, I bought it and began my career as a landlord.

The Candler Park area in Atlanta was on the cusp of renewal. My third purchase was a duplex that resembled Dr. Schweitzer's first medical compound in Lamborene. I could imagine the natives coming out of high grasses to see the good doctor on his wide wooden porch. B, in some puzzlement and hauteur, said: "How will you ever make money on that?" But I did. The listing agent suggested that I should get my own real estate license so that I could recoup some commission on sales. When people asked me about this strange avocation, I replied that some professionals played golf to relax. I did real estate. And was it really all that diverse from religion? The latter urges us to be of service to our neighbor. Helping someone find shelter without being cheated seemed noble enough. And I liked the suspense and serendipity of being an entrepreneur.

As a landlord with other things to do, I depended on property managers, handymen and reasonably sane tenants to keep it all going. There were times of major frustration, especially with my factotum handymen who often drove me to distraction. But I also came to appreciate in them the virtues of working class life. Yet I couldn't afford and did not want to be an absentee landlord. I enjoyed the physical work and found that I had unknown skills to fix things. Not many religion professors have had to disarm a mentally disturbed tenant coming at them with a sharp letter opener because he thought I was the one who pushed him down the stairs at the factory. I was sorry to have to hurl him through a sheet rock wall, but he wasn't hurt. Peggy reminds me that I took her on one of our first dates to a landfill in my pickup truck loaded with property discards.

Nothing brings us down to earth like the deaths of those close to us. C's sudden passing in 1984 seemed like an injustice in the evolutionary order. This woman, eleven years my junior, was not supposed to die in her early forties, especially not by her own hand, as it were. It wasn't a suicide in the ordinary sense, but it was self-induced through alcohol. I thought of her loneliness and depression in that last stage when her then husband left. Our marriage was tumultuous and often impossible. Yet I had a dream about her the night before I got the news of her death. She was relating to me with affection.

Her leaving pitched me into the strongest depression of my life. I felt betrayed and abandoned. Yet our early love was a first for both of us. In a strange way, it hovered in the stillness beneath the storms of our lives. I will never know the extent of her inner pain from childhood. Her many starts and stops were attempts to cope with that origin. I wished that she would have reached out to therapists in San Luis Obispo, to someone who could have helped her examine patterns of seeking external change as an escape from taking care of her lost inner child. I wrote in my journal: "C, we had hard times but happy ones, too. I don't know what happened in your years with A, but I have feelings of love for you. I hope you are at peace now, and that we will meet in God. I cry for your death, but I smile for your lively spirit."

1988: INTERVIEW WITH PRESIDENT CARTER ON AGING

8

Things Fall Apart and Come Together

The seed of God is in us.
Given an intelligent and hardworking farmer,
it will . . . grow up to God.

—MEISTER ECKHART

IN 1988 I WAS sitting on the deck of my home with my standard poodle, Jenny, wondering about another tough transition. A third marriage had ended, and a good friend, John Delury, had died suddenly of a heart attack. I had known John since high school. He represented the intelligence and wit of the best type of Catholic layman. It was a time of endings. In my late fifties, I was counting the years from my own terminus. As I sat quietly looking out into sun-drenched oak trees, I reflected that all this change could have spiritual meaning, if I learned to sit still and listen. Taoist and Buddhist meditations helped me see life from a contemplative center. My new course in ecology and religion made me more conscious of my links to earth. Nature was pointing toward a vast spirituality that transcended the limits of religious institutions.

I cared about these institutions because they impacted people for good or ill. But I had also outgrown them in important ways. I respected them as training camps on the spiritual path, but I was coming to see their rules and belief systems in new ways. Their teachings represented moral guidelines and imaginative metaphors. Yet I had to make decisions about these heritages for myself, while I was learning about life from life, or better, from life shocks.

I thought about events over which I had partial influence at best. I was learning that the concrete happenings of our lives deeply shape our spiritual understanding. It was all too easy to just do the practices of religion and speak the traditional words. We could delude ourselves into concluding that such conduct defined one's religion. Yet spirit life was also powerfully embedded in my emotional experiences. Marital struggles and challenges in the workplace tested my self-understanding. These events both humbled and invited me to fathom their meaning for myself. Unanswered questions kept surfacing. After three failed marriages, was I capable of real intimacy? Was I developing a broader religiousness without being able to name it? Did my writing on aging have any relation to my personal life? Was I wasting my time writing a novel that would not be seen as serious in academic circles? I had no clear answers, only more questions. But I was convinced that any authentic responses would come from keeping my ear to the ground of inner wisdom.

By the late eighties, I realized how much of a collector, or possibly "connector," I am. I don't hoard material things, but I cultivate old connections with my history. I even "collect" former wives when they allow it. I don't like to burn bridges. My recurrent "Jesuit dream" emphasizes this tendency in its focus on belonging and cutting ties. In many forms, it's story line is about leaving the order. Should I go or stay? Women, jobs, my family of origin as well as Jesuit friends cluster around this transition. The emotions of the dream are so intense at times that I am amazed to wake up with a wife of sixteen years beside me in bed. The dream feelings were so troubling that I was pleased to awake and know that I didn't have to go through those earlier transitions. Since leaving the order in 1968, I have stayed in touch with Jesuit friends. My wife says I'm still a Jesuit in disguise. The Pope would probably doubt or deny that I can be considered a Catholic in good standing. But there are links deeper than the measurable categories for being a Catholic. Certain tenacious sensibilities and outlooks from the tradition linger, especially with the order. These become a kind of secret handshake, even though I can disagree with teachings and practices of the church and of the Society of Jesus.

So it has been with my wives. C died in 1984, but we had a few contacts after our breakup in 1974. V's temperament was reclusive. She chose to distance herself from me. But B has been a remarkable example of close friendship after a difficult marriage. It defies logic in light of the tortured situation of our years as husband and wife. Some would say that old pressures of marriage dissolved. There certainly is some truth in this. But at another level, we still love each other. I remind my wife, Peggy, who has been the most gracious and non-jealous of partners, that love is not a zero-sum game. Her retort is to smile and lift a quizzical eye while commenting on my jesuitical rationalizing.

Peggy was understanding about my personal history and my hasty tendencies. She was reassuring about us. There was to be no rush to the altar. George advised me not to marry ever. This was not a judgment about Peggy. He was underscoring my limited talents in the spousal realm. He foresaw me at seventy trapped in an unhappy relationship or again divorced. On the tenth anniversary of our wedding, George complimented me, admitting that he didn't think he would see this milestone, given my earlier proclivities. Of course, there was sexual attraction with Peggy, but more importantly, in the three years before marriage, we established a close friendship. My earlier marriages were hurried by the glow of initial feelings without giving myself time to recognize negative signs.

It's hard to compare relationships because they happen at different ages and life situations. When we married in 1993, Peggy was more mature than my previous wives. Hopefully, I was, too. But a key factor was Peggy's calm acceptance of herself. Because she was less needy in terms of her own self-esteem, she was more capable of loving me as I am. She was less sexually demanding, accepting and finding pleasure as we were. To a large extent, this restored my own sense of self-confidence on the intimate level. It underlies what I wrote in my journal after our third year together: "Peggy is a blessing in my life. I love her for herself and want her life with me to be very good." When I see lines like that many years later, I'm tempted to curb their idealism by saying that we've had our moments. But the underlying cadence of our relationship has been a loving embrace of the other's inner being.

These reflections on marriage emphasize growth through concrete experiences. Again we are back to touchstone events of life as ways of shifting us into deeper assessments of self and world. I find a similar pattern of learning through inner experience to be true in my academic life. If I had conformed very closely to criteria for advancement at the university, I might have attained a chaired or distinguished professorship. I know that I could have performed according to the more restrictive norms of research and writing. I might have chosen a very limited topic to become a scholar who knew as much as anyone else about the subject, and perhaps a tad more. Yet I doubt that I would have been enthusiastic about such a limited range of inquiry. I would have been denying my true interests arising from inner criteria. I would have been sacrificing wider projects that appealed to my soul in order to climb further on the academic ladder.

Writing on the spirituality of aging and of ecology, topics that excited me and seemed to be socially important, would not measure up in the eyes of peer judges who held a more confined vision of scholarship. My kind of writing could get me to full professorship, but not a coveted chaired professorship. For example, had I been driven by the goal of a named professorship, I might have focused on someone like Arne Naess, the Norwegian philosopher of deep ecology. I could have placed all my research into such a limited topic, perhaps even learning Norwegian. I would have imitated the research process of other highly regarded scholars who staked their professional lives on a Sartre or Kierkegaard. But I would have been denying inner impulses, motivations deriving from personal experience. I wouldn't have launched into research on subjects where I thought I could make a valuable contribution.

In the early eighties, I saw that scholars of religion had largely neglected issues concerning aging. I realized that much of the literature on middle age and later life, as it pertained to the field of religious studies, focused on superficial surveys about church attendance among elders. As I look back on this period, I see that I was doing two things that seemed personally meaningful. In my own mid-life, I wanted to learn how to age well. The cryptic words of Teilhard de Chardin kept coming back, *il faut finir bien.* It was important for me personally to finish life as best I could. How could I deal creatively with my own anxieties about death? How could life be meaningful after retirement? Secondly, I wanted to say something that could be helpful to an expanding population of elders. These promptings stemmed also from my Jesuit background, that impulse of Ignatius toward the *cura animarum,* the care of souls. As a modern person, I was less interested than he in a care system that got people to heaven. But in fairness to Ignatius, he was also concerned about bettering life on earth.

My three books on aging build on people's experiences as well as related literature in psychology and spirituality. *Aging as a Spiritual Journey* didn't have much competition when it appeared in the early eighties. Few works went beyond rudimentary surveys on religion and aging. I could have written my new book from studies in psychology and religion. But it would have been more of a theoretical essay. I wanted it to reflect the real experiences of older people. I chose to interview persons with backgrounds in institutional religion and the academy. I talked with them about links between their personal religiousness and the aging process. These men and women were a generation ahead of me. A few had been my own mentors. This research became a way of reflecting on my own aging. The wisdom of these remarkable people as they met the challenges of life inspired me to see my own older age in a positive light.

About a decade later in *Elder Wisdom*, I intensified the interview process, but with a more "secular" style. In *Aging as a Spiritual Journey*, I often discussed issues in traditional theological language. This way of speaking was comfortable for interviewees who had lived in close contact with institutional religion. They could talk about the cross or salvation in light of their life experiences. But in *Elder Wisdom*, I wanted to focus on spirituality implicit in what we consider to be secular life. I like to think that this attempt to close the commonly accepted divide between the sacred and the secular has been a hallmark of my thinking. For example, my book, *The Religious Experience of Revolutionaries*, underscored this theme in the early seventies. Whatever was sacred had to be immersed in the secular, the here and now. We talked in terms of the virtues of aging well, such as gratitude and acceptance, among many other qualities that stemmed from life experiences. I understand the critique of my position, which asks for a clearer distinction between secular and sacred. But I would rather sin on the side of melding these categories, leaning on the Jesuit motto of finding God in all things.

My third book of short meditations on aging, *On Growing Older*, represents my own revived interest in contemplative life. I was seeing more clearly that the "pay dirt" of religion, its deepest realms had to do with mysticism, direct contact with the transcendent in the world. It's regrettable that most institutional religions do not emphasize the contemplative life. For the most part, these traditions are fearful of mysticism, in part because hierarchs find it hard to control. The idea of mysticism seems very remote to most ostensibly religious people. They associate it with John of the Cross and other contemplative virtuosos without realizing that everyone has mystical potential. Religious ethics, how we treat one another and the planet, are always vitally important, but such morality needs the contemplative to remain authentic. Without the listening wisdom and self-corrective of meditation, ethical judgments and actions can easily slip into self- and group justification. Study and practice in Buddhism and Taoism brought me back to Western mysticism.

Focus on the experiential and contemplative influenced my choice of new courses and how I taught them. Much to my satisfaction, the

Religion Department at Emory supported novel courses. My course on death and dying was one of the earlier offerings in this genre. On the intellectual level, students discovered plenty of reading and critical reflection. But I also had them keep journals not only about assigned authors, but also about their own reactions. I brought in films and speakers that elicited emotions around the subject of death. One film was a documentary about the dying of a black minister. We also presented a panel on HIV-AIDS with professionals who treated afflicted persons. These most often would be young men closer to the age of the students. Before the advances of today's medications, such a person faced death in the near future. The films and panels were themselves a kind of contemplation. Student journals fostered meditative reflection on crucial topics and connected intellect with emotion. Although the course required a good deal of work, it was well attended for many years.

My course on dreams and spiritual meaning derived from my immersion in Jungian psychology after the collapse of my first marriage. My therapist had me record and reflect on my dreams, especially their emotional valence. How might the narratives and metaphors of these sleeping events point me into fuller knowledge of my personal history? I wasn't trying to turn a course with undergraduates into personal therapy. Rather I saw it as a way to open students to imaginative and metaphorical dimensions in their own lives. In some ways, it reflected a creative writing course with material coming out of their own imaginations. I gave them methods to follow in their dream journals, which became copious reading for me at the semester's end. Students learned something about the psychology of dreaming and how religious traditions understood visions and dreams. The students also became aware of recurrent dreams and, especially, their emotional impact. They were beginning to open their "doors of perception," in the words of Aldous Huxley. It taught them that religion and spirituality were not mainly about things outside themselves.

My course on ecology and religion followed similar directions. I drew readings from Eastern and Western wisdom traditions as well as nature writings from Thoreau to contemporary "Deep Ecology." We studied world religions to ask how well or badly they related to environmental needs. We tried to understand how we might interpret central teachings of these heritages in ecologically beneficial ways. Again, I used student journals to assure that they were reading at least some of the material and appropriating it in critical and personal ways. Every class would conclude with a guided meditation drawn from a significant theme of the day. Each class began with a few Chi Gong exercises to summon the students away from distractedness. It was a way of making them aware of their contact with nature through attention to breathing. My standard poodle, Jenny, became a regular visitor to class when we were discussing relationships between humans and animals. On a good weather day, we walked down a ravine on campus to a stream where we meditated on trees, water, sun, and wildlife. We attempted to move beyond concepts to tactile and emotional contact with self and earth. Nature itself could become a temple for finding interconnectedness and the transcendent. I was pleased to have been able to start a new section in the American Academy of Religion on ecology and religion that endures to this day. The AAR is the main professional guild for professors of religious studies.

A final course that I continued for five years after retirement was "Christianity Meets Buddhism," focusing on contemplatives in each tradition. I added Taoist themes through the *Tao Te Ching*. I was giving the course as much for myself as for the students. The material spoke powerfully to my own spiritual needs. I became convinced that the subject matter would help me along my road to *finir bien*. I chose readings from mentors like Thich Nhat Hanh, Anthony de Mello and others who linked the contemplative paths of both traditions. Again I used Chi Gong exercises to start class and guided meditation to end it. There was plenty of time in between to discuss students' weekly papers. I began the course with Jon Kabat-Zinn's *Wherever You Go, There You Are*, which is one of the best introductions to meditation. This Jewish therapist draws on many spiritual traditions to lead the initiate along the path and into the stream.

At this time I was learning Tai Chi with a Chinese master who worked at Emory as a scientific investigator. Dr. Xu was extraordinarily thorough, but very slow in his instructions. With the help of my colleague Carl Brown, a biologist, I finally learned to do Yang Style Long Form with a group of six adults who continue to meet weekly for the practice. With my undergraduates, the Chi Gong exercises introduced them to meditative movement in place. Tai Chi carries such movements into a wider dance of martial arts turned inward. I don't think we have anything in the West (except perhaps walking the labyrinth) that approximates Tai Chi. These movements combine body in motion with patterned breathing and the quieting of monkey mind for contemplative experience. I find it an ideal exercise for earth religion as opposed to the sky religion of concepts and beliefs. Ignatian meditation, with its contemplation of place, aims to draw the meditator into an imaginative, sensual scene. But it lacks bodily movement, making it harder for the contemplative person to avoid falling into concepts, or even falling asleep, as I recall from my days in Jesuit training on a hard kneeler in early morning hours.

It has been four decades since I left the Jesuits and my professional status as a Roman Catholic priest. Was I still a Catholic or even a Christian in light of my involvements with Eastern religions and my new ways of thinking about theology? This question has many aspects and defies easy answers. It comes up periodically in my journals and calls forth partial responses along the way. In the late sixties and early seventies it was easier to see myself as a married Catholic priest bent on reforming the church, even though it did not recognize Latin rite married priests, except some converts from the Anglican and Lutheran communions. I thought then and still do that a key to serious reform of the church was the elimination of mandated celibacy for priests. It surely wasn't the only important element for reform, but without optional celibacy, the centuries-old, sclerotic networks of the Vatican would grind along in the same old grooves. There had to be a radical lifestyle change in leadership to move the church beyond control by a self-protective celibate caste. My role as first president of the Society of Priests for a Free Ministry in 1969 symbolized this conviction. But we had to do more than intellectualize about such reform. We had to make it happen by doing ministries, even eucharistic ones, with like-minded persons, despite Vatican protests.

There were a number of rationales behind SPFM. One was the argument that the church had a married clergy for its first thousand years. It has also had an informally "married clergy" during its second millennium from the love children of cardinals to the secret and not so secret common-law wives, especially of rural priests. We could lean on the old argument that if something has existed, it could come to be again. This was a good argument against the opposition who tried to uphold the present clerical system as the fixed will of God. We were also convinced that most priests would be happier and more effective if they didn't have to battle the demands of celibacy. While I understand the medieval reasons for imposing celibacy on the priesthood, I see it as a great historical aberration that has caused much unnecessary suffering for priests and for women related to them. Moreover, removing the rule of celibacy today would enlarge the talent pool of new recruits to the ministry.

SPFM soon called for the priestly ordination of women, a stronger challenge to church tradition than married male priests. In some ways, this became clearer to us as women became intimates in our lives. The church was only hurting itself by excluding them from priestly ministry with theologically weak reasons. It's noteworthy today to see the almost visceral anger and quick rejection of the Vatican toward women's ordination. Rome buries its head in the sand when confronted by better arguments in its favor. We could learn much from the experience of women priests in the Episcopal tradition. Although SPFM was not talking about democracy at the start, it became clearer that such structural changes constituted a movement away from oligarchy towards a people-oriented church. The rule of the celibate few, we thought, must give way to wider participation of Christians.

These themes were taken up in a book I did with Rosemary Ruether, *A Democratic Catholic Church*. We were collaborating again. It had been twenty years since our joint effort, *From Machismo to Mutuality*. In the democracy book, we were looking beyond issues of celibacy and feminism. The Roman Church has been resistant to democratizing movements. This is understandable since the church came to be in a culture of imperial absolutism. The Catholic Church resisted the development of liberal democracies in Europe during the nineteenth century. It also fought intellectual and scientific dimensions of the Enlightenment. Progressives and anti-clericals saw the Roman Church as a bastion of the monarchical-aristocratic world that was fading away. The first openings to democratic polity in official Catholicism came only at Vatican II, especially with its new teaching on religious liberty. The architect of this movement was an intellectual hero of mine, John Courtney Murray, SJ. I find it coincidently interesting that he received an honorary degree from Columbia University in 1966 at the commencement where I received a PhD. I value the photo we took together that day, and I was honored to be asked to write an article in recent years for *The Way, the British Journal of Spirituality* (October, 2004) commemorating his important contributions.

John Courtney Murray used a phrase that might well characterize my kind of Catholicism. He talked about "becoming unstuck" from
ideas and institutions that once seemed dominant and unchangeable. I
could still be a Catholic and disagree on many moral issues, especially
those relating to sexuality such as birth control, homosexuality, divorce,
and even abortion. These are finally ethical issues, although conservative
interpreters would argue that divorce and homosexuality are forbidden
in the New Testament. Yet the church has no special wisdom on such
matters. These are topics of right and wrong that develop through the
trial-and-error mode of human consciousness in historical circumstances. But the church does claim to have God-given and unchangeable beliefs about doctrines like the Trinity and the divinity of Jesus. Of
course, such claims are also true of other Christian churches.

But "becoming unstuck" meant for me following my best insights
and convictions about the impact of historical conditioning on even
these key doctrines. To put my position in a nutshell, I would say that
we can't really think like fourth-century theologians whose councils
solidified claims about Christ's divinity and the Holy Trinity. We can
understand how it was possible and even relatively easy for these earlier
thinkers to divinize a human. This happened commonly with Roman
emperors and the leaders of other religious movements. The contro-
versies about Jesus's divinity were also intense political struggles within
early Christianity, as well as in the early church's struggles with competing pagan religions. The early church's claim that Jesus is God's unique
and final revelation enhanced the power of hierarchs and the institution
itself. Bishops were on the verge of becoming major secular leaders in
important cities. Constantine did not want a weak God in Jesus Christ.
It would not support his reasons of state for choosing Christianity as
religion of empire.

Of course, this is not the whole story about the first centuries of
Christianity concerning central doctrines like the divinity of Christ and
the Trinity. These Christian teachings are great metaphorical or mythopoetic attempts to imagine and define the human relationship with the
ultimately unknowable mystery of God. Both teachings say that God
is immersed in an unfolding universe. Beliefs also codify church order
and worship. Scholars today, however, are finding competing views of
other early Christians, such as the Gnostics, who differed with orthodox
understandings of doctrine. Their newly discovered writings or gospels

challenge the interpretations that won out in the early councils. These gospels were suppressed and their authors called heretics.

But I return to my point above that it isn't really possible for me and many other Christians to think like fourth-century theologians. Why is this so? Because a revolution of consciousness has happened in the West from Copernicus to String Theory and from Galileo to Darwin and onward. Catholic "Geologian," Thomas Berry writes impressively about this change of consciousness in his evolutionary grasp of revelation. I wouldn't say that controversial Jesuit theologian, Roger Haight, agrees with my conclusions, but in *Jesus, Symbol of God* he, too, is aware of the changed perspective of the twenty-first century-mind. Early Christian thinkers didn't have a clue about cosmic vastness or the millions of years of human evolution. Nor did Ignatius and Luther in the sixteenth century. For them the heavenly bodies seemed not so far away, and Adam and Eve were understood as a human couple who lived only countable generations before. The earth, however oddly conceived, was the center of the cosmos. Religious thinkers and churches could make huge claims that seem preposterous today. Such inherent problems aren't answered by a simple recourse to having faith. That just obscures the issue for a good-faith modern mind. Moreover, faith is not primarily about clinging to a list of beliefs. It's more like an agnostic openness and trust toward the ever mysterious transcendent. Luther had it right about faith as a form of trust or confidence in God.

Does this view of things leave me without spiritual moorings? Not at all. But I will have to say more about being an ecumenical, metaphorical, historical and agnostic Catholic Christian. Why do I even want to maintain an identity as a Catholic? One reason is that the spirituality I have been describing is compatible with being a Catholic, especially in the implied "catholic" or universal sense of the religion. Most people tend to reduce being a Catholic to observing certain rules and rituals. This can certainly be part of Catholic identity. But it is not the only way to adhere to this tradition. One can be grasped in faith by wider aspects of the heritage: the powerful attraction of Jesus's inspiration as lived by many saints (and I don't limit that word to canonized saints) in the church. This might be considered the communitarian or family belonging aspect of Catholicism. I have had the privilege of living with some of those saints. Their spirit has been contagious. It may help here to distinguish beliefs from a deeper sense of belonging. Very few Catholics could go far in explaining such beliefs as Trinity, Incarnation or salvation. These and other theological doctrines are worthy metaphorical and imaginative ways of talking about the mystery of Christianity. But they are secondary to experiencing the roots of the tradition.

This is how I would differ from Garry Wills, the outstanding historian and public intellectual, in his book, *Why I Am a Catholic*. Following his mentor, Chesterton, Wills stresses beliefs about the papacy and the Apostle's Creed to undergird his Catholicism. I honor his approach, but I don't think it goes deep enough. Sociologists of religion, like Rodney Stark, have shown empirically that people identify with a church tradition not mainly because of beliefs, but rather because they find a spiritual home or community. It's more like belonging to a family than working out an intellectual calculus. Hans Küng, in *Why I Am Still a Christian*, comes closer to my position by invoking the "Spirit of Jesus Christ who is alive today." He envisages a community and communities that embody this Jesus spirit in radically humane ways of justice, peace and compassion. It is a spiritual humanism that embraces the positive and negative dimensions of humanity. Like Küng, I think this can be done within the Catholic Church at its ecumenical best.

In the words of philosopher Charles Taylor: "Vatican rule-makers and secularist ideologies unite in not being able to see that there are more ways of being a Catholic Christian than either have yet imagined." (From a review of *A Secular Age*, in *National Catholic Reporter*.) Taylor is calling for a fuller way of expanding Catholic imagination and identity. In *Practicing Catholic*, James Carroll says that he left the priesthood to become a writer who could both critique the church and also open up its imaginative richness to shape an adequate Catholic identity. He attempts to show how a "basic understanding of faith as rooted in imagination and expression can brace every Catholic's identity. My assumption has been that one Catholic personal journey can illuminate the pathways taken by—and now open to—all." (From *Practicing Catholic*.)

In the context I described above (of an ecumenical, metaphorical, agnostic Catholic Christian), I have been moving in an Arian direction on Jesus for some time. I discussed Arius of Alexandria as a major theologian of the fourth century. In brief, he portrayed Jesus as an extraordinary human but not divine as in the sense of the Second Person of the Trinity. In following this view, I have been greatly helped in recent decades by the group of New Testament scholars called The Jesus Seminar, also referred to as the latest quest for the historical Jesus. Among these researchers, I would single out John Dominic Crossan, Marcus Borg and Robert Funk. I'm not saying that everyone in this historical quest school would end up with my position.

Perhaps Borg summarizes Jesus best as a charismatic Jewish teacher, a God-obsessed mystic, a healer, a social prophet, a Hebrew reformer and the inspirer of a new movement. His central message about the Kingdom or domain of God had interior and exterior ramifications. It meant the ability to become transformed in the here and now toward a life of charity and justice. It required a recurrent *metanoia* or change of heart whereby we become aware of our excessive desires and their negative consequences for society (a very Buddhist idea, by the way). The Kingdom of God summons us to build peaceable communities in a strife-torn world. Thus Jesus was called Prince of Peace.

But what about his divinity? He was seen by his disciples as a God-filled or holy person. He was divine in the ways that we are all divine, only more so. I see the difference between his divinity and ours as a matter of degree not kind. Therefore, I don't think Jesus was God in the fullest, most absolute sense as understood in the doctrine of the Trinity. I like the phrase that God was in Jesus as a splendid human exemplar of divinity. We all have the potential to become Christs, each in our own way. This resembles the Buddhist teaching that we all have Buddha-nature within, and it can be more fully realized in the course of our lives.

> I say more: the just man justices;
> Keeps grace: that keeps all his goings graces;
> Acts in God's eye what in God's eye he is—
> Christ. For Christ plays in ten thousand places,
> Lovely in limbs, and lovely in eyes not his
> To the Father through the features of men's faces.

—GERARD MANLEY HOPKINS, "AS KINGFISHERS CATCH FIRE"

When I think about orthodox positions on the divinity of Christ, I am more and more struck by the vast mystery surrounding these claims. Many believers have come to accept this teaching on faith, as they say, without reflecting much on the limits of our knowledge, even when we resort to a faith commitment as justification. There it is, take it or leave it. Yet we know that more proximate mysteries like the relationship between mind and brain puzzle scientists. Some scientists think that the ultimate resolution of such issues may be beyond our ken.

I don't use this analogy to question Jesus's divinity-humanity as though this teaching was on the same level as scientific knowing. Rather I bring it up to highlight the even greater chasm in our knowing about the nature of God in Jesus (our essential agnosticism). All I draw from these comparisons is an imperative for humility in what we can assert, a kind of respectful "not-knowing" that would tolerate or even encourage plural understandings of how God could be in Jesus and in us. We might be inclined then within Christianity to honor those who are drawn to a lower or a higher Christology. This attitude would be closer, I think, to the diversity of thought on the topic in the church of the first centuries.

My views are hardly novel. An Arian strain has been present in Christianity from the beginning. It can be found not only among early Arian Christians, but in the Gnostic gospels that had wide currency in the early centuries, and were suppressed by the organizers of the canonical New Testament in the third century. The documents discovered at Nag Hammadi, Egypt, in the 1940s attest to such early tenets. For the first three hundred years. Christian communities followed a number of different gospels that brought out various aspects of Jesus. These groups managed to live peacefully with one another for the most part. Gregory Riley in *One Jesus, Many Christs* notes the diversity of beliefs in the early period. He argues that the Greco-Roman idea of the hero was more salient in antiquity than later belief systems. Christian communities understood Jesus as the ultimate religious hero though they had quite variant views of whether he was divine. They differed on other beliefs such as the Trinity and the importance of the resurrection.

The Socinian movement in Poland in the sixteenth and seventeenth centuries held that Jesus did not exist until he was created as a human being. In this belief they emphasized Christ's humanity even more than the early church Arians. Socinians were quite influential in Europe until they were banished from Poland by the Catholic Church in 1638. Unitarianism in England and in eighteenth-century New England became an heir of this long tradition. Founders of the American republic like Jefferson, Adams, Madison, and Franklin, as Enlightenment thinkers, came to share the Arian bent as they praised aspects of Jesus's ethics while dispensing with what they called supernaturalism or superstition. The Quaker movement also rejected orthodox theology about a God dying on the cross to atone for our sins in favor of embracing Jesus's teaching of the Kingdom of God within us, led by the Holy Spirit.

Traditional Christian eucharistic liturgies in mainline churches still enshrine the divinity of Jesus in the fullest sense. When I attend these services in Catholic and Episcopalian churches, I find spiritual meaning in various aspects of the liturgy, but I also demythologize the high Christology or see it metaphorically. I don't recite the first part of the Nicene Creed. I would have to push what I can do as a metaphorical Christian beyond what my conscience would allow to say that Jesus is God of God, begotten before all things were made. I can pick up again with "I believe in the communion of saints."

For some years, Peggy and I participated in a house-church movement in Atlanta called Emmaus. We did a eucharistic liturgy every second Sunday led by the hosts of a particular home. These liturgies are creatively designed by local leaders. They maintain much of the form of traditional liturgies as well as the seasonal feasts. But the creeds and prayers present a more human Jesus. At these gatherings, I appreciated the face to face sharing of long-time friends dwelling on the gospels and other readings in light of their own lives. Emmaus does a potluck lunch after each liturgy, a continuation of holy communion. This experience makes me wonder why skilled liturgists in the Catholic and other churches don't explore a more fundamental reform of the liturgy, one that would be more in keeping with the contemporary mind. I am not opposed to conservatives worshipping in the old Latin rite, if they find spiritual meaning in it. But what Jesus said about the Sabbath can be said about the liturgy: it is for humans and not the other way around.

These thoughts on liturgies call for a few more reflections on being a metaphorical, agnostic Christian. All theology is a form of mythology. I'm using myth in a positive sense, the way it's treated in literary studies. The very word, "theology," means conversation about God. But God is ultimately unknowable to us. Therefore, agnosticism is the only realistic position for a critically thinking person. An ancient apophatic tradition in Christianity respected the ultimate mystery of God and stressed that God can only be known as not this and not that, by none of the limiting categories of human experience and knowledge. Mystics know this in all religious heritages. (The great Hindu theologian, Sankara, used the Sanskrit words, "neti, neti" to underscore his agnosticism: "not this, not that.") Since we are all potential mystics, it shouldn't be too hard for us to grasp this theme. All seemingly positive affirmations about God are at best just fingers pointing toward God from a long way off. Even these statements about God are subject to constant review and re-thinking in keeping with new insights in the course of history. We do the best we can with our mythopoetic metaphors in theology, but it's a great mistake to think that these lofty imaginings (e.g., Trinity) are clearly descriptive of their object or that they are set once and for all as irreformable truth.

The *Tao Te Ching* emphasizes the spiritual value of not-knowing. A major task of the Taoist master is to lead people toward not-knowing. Only then, in the experience of not-knowing, can they become open to their true source, the Tao, within humanity and beyond it. So, being an agnostic Catholic means being a critically thinking Catholic. It should not be confused with atheism. As an agnostic, I have faith or trust in God while recognizing the severe limits of my knowing the divine. Wise agnosticism is demanded by the nature of religious language. Paul Tillich warned against the mistake of turning myth into hard and fast history. This is the constant fundamentalist temptation. It produces false certainty, even though it may console people with a feeling of security. The authentic religious seeker is called to live on a riskier edge. In an odd way, atheists tend to be fundamentalists on the other end of the spectrum. They assert the non-existence of God without allowing for indicators that may point to transcendent experience (the contemplative life) or partial, very limited knowledge of the divine. Atheists need to become better agnostics about their own arguments.

But why should I care about being identified as a Catholic Christian in a metaphorical and agnostic way? Why not drop the tradition as irrelevant to my life now? Before attempting to answer these questions, I respect another's choice to leave the Catholic Church. Some do it out of alienation, others to find a more adequate spiritual home. From what I have written, many Catholics would probably say that I have already in fact left the church. Be that as it may, a combination of personal choice and historical circumstance incline me to embrace the Catholic heritage. I certainly don't think it is the one, true church or the unique vehicle of salvation, a word that I would mainly describe in a this-worldly sense of living according to the virtues/insights of Jesus and other spiritual masters. I can argue against the sclerotic structure and many teachings of the hierarchy (Benedictine Philip Kaufman, expressed the value of such dissent in: *Why You Can Disagree and Remain a Faithful Catholic*). Yet I am uplifted spiritually by Jesus's lifestyle and teachings, as well as by much else in the gospels, in the contemplative tradition and in the lives of saints, old and new.

But there is also the aspect of historical circumstance. I could after all join another church and identify as a Methodist or Episcopalian, for example, and still be motivated by much of the same Christian tradition. Yet our callings have a particularity. Because of where I've found myself, both in and out of the Society of Jesus, I've sensed a vocation to work as a reformer from within the Catholic tradition, while seeking wisdom from many heritages, Western and Eastern. In this sense, I can also define myself as Unitarian Catholic or a Taoist-Buddhist Catholic. I'm sure this will bother not a few Catholics and non-Catholics. They will accuse me of not thinking straight or of being a wishy-washy, liberal dilettante. But how can I deny the valuable insights and practices that I've learned from Buddhism and Taoism? These are part of me now. I would be content to die with Buddhist and Christian phrases on my lips. I think about Marcus Borg's little book about Jesus and Buddha as brothers. On my meditation table, I have Japanese and Tibetan gongs, a Russian icon of Mary and Jesus, a south Asian sitting Buddha, accompanied by pictures of Clare and Francis of Assisi. They all seem to get along just fine. I admire Martin Luther for the path he chose. But I also esteem Desiderius Erasmus for his choice to reform the Catholic Church.

All these themes mesh with concrete happenings of my life on the ground, as it were. The central positive event of this period was my marriage to Peggy Herrman on May Day, 1993 under a native maple on our land on the Oconee River. It has been a great mental and physical benefit to me to find a partner who shares my life on many levels, including spiritual involvements. My other wives were good women each in her own way. Personality clashes, different life scripts, and other shortcomings drew us apart. Could it have been otherwise? In the abstract, the answer would be yes, but life isn't lived in the abstract. We move forward in the brokenness of the historical present. I'm grateful for continuing connections. C carried my picture in her wallet when she died. And B has been a lasting friendship that couldn't have been predicted.

I'll conclude this chapter with a few memories of *eros* and *thanatos*, love-feasts and the deaths of special people. We tend to restrict *eros* too exclusively to sexual love. But eating together may be one of our highest pleasures. The nurture of food and conversation builds and sustains community. Two images from this time stand out in memory. They both reflect the open table that scholars point to in the life of Jesus. Meals can be understandably confined to immediate family and friends. But there are examples of more inclusive community. For some time I volunteered to help with breakfast on Sundays at the Open Door Community in Atlanta where street people were fed, lodged and clothed. The Open Door is a Protestant extension of the older Catholic Worker movement, inspired by Peter Maurin and Dorothy Day. As I mentioned earlier, I became the gray-haired grits man, ladling this southern polenta out of a huge pot. Without trying to romanticize the homeless with their hard existence on the streets and their personal problems, it was an experience of the open table. It was also for me an occasion of questioning my motives for getting involved. Was I just expiating liberal guilt for my comfortable status as a college professor? Did I want to look good in the eyes of peers who would note my generosity? My old Jesuit training with its concern about the poor played into it. In the end, I concluded that most of our actions stem from mixed inspirations. Of greater significance was the experience of eating/conversing with persons across social lines. This communication was usually limited, but it was a start at sharing a common humanity over bacon, eggs and coffee.

Taking meals together is usually done in a perfunctory way. It amounts to routine refueling. I'm as guilty of this as anyone. But occasionally a spiritual teacher like Thich Nhat Hanh reminds us about awareness in the ordinary activities of the day. At meals this attentiveness is not only for personal contemplation or for health purposes, but also for conviviality, for the pleasure of company with others. Another example of an open table struck me when Peggy and I visited my Italian cousins in the hills outside of the port town of Chiavari in Liguria. For Luisa, my first cousin, a good part of the day revolved around a big kitchen. Her husband, Angelo, a slate roof contractor continually invited guests to take more food and drink. The operative word here is "guests." The long table seemed to attract extended family, local priests, roofing co-workers, neighbors and special friends. They just seemed to drop in during the mid-day dinner. I don't think they phoned ahead. They just stopped by, knowing that Luisa would offer them something to accompany a glass of wine. It didn't matter much whether my cousins really liked the opportunistic visitor. There probably was a silent rural ritual guiding these comings and goings, but it wasn't obvious.

When we got to Siena on the same trip, a Eucharistic Congress was in progress. From what I could see in the program, none of the clerical speakers related holy communion to common meals. It was all about the Mass, the rite where Jesus makes himself symbolically present in bread and wine. This sacramental meal, controlled by clerics, was seen as something apart from ordinary life. It was presented as a holier event. But I think that Jesus, who according to gospel stories, liked to dine, would have found holy eating and holy communion in the Open Door Community and in Luisa's kitchen. Symbolic rites like the Mass certainly have a place in religious movements. But I don't think they are any more holy than a pleasurable meal among friends. Sky religion tends to lift rites above the terrestrial to an almost immaterial sphere. The tasteless wafer at Mass can hardly be recognized as bread. The eucharistic service reduces natural bread to a distant symbol. Again, there was no mention in the conference about the relationship between Eucharist and the ecological plight of the earth. It wouldn't take much imagination to go from grain and grape to the planet that nurtures them. This is an example of why religious institutions are important. When they are alive to the spirit of earth, they can become vehicles for vital transformation. But when they are lost in conventional ritual, they squander their potential.

In 2007 a group of Dutch Dominicans circulated a booklet, "Church and Ministry," that justified lay people presiding at the Eucharist. Such celebrations have been going on for years in "house churches" among Catholics around the world, but this may be the first time that official clergy have openly proposed the possibility. The Dutch theologians say that the priest shortage justifies a return to an old tradition that associates the Eucharist to local communities. We see here a democratizing of this ritual. These Dominicans bring needed attention to the vital place of the community "from below" in understanding the Eucharist.

On the question of eating, Peggy and I went vegetarian for a couple of years. This was partly inspired by health reasons, but also motivated by wanting to do less harm to animals and to the earth. A chronic fatigue syndrome urged Peggy back to consuming animal protein and I followed suit. The experiment taught us that we could live well, maybe even better, with a much reduced intake of meat. It also continues to make us conscious of the ecological problems of grazing so many animals, and keeps us aware of the unnecessary cruelty of factory farming. For this reason we don't eat veal. We also regularly thank the animal whose flesh we are consuming in the manner of American Indians. These are small measures but they keep us mindful. In recent years, I have developed a quirky habit of not killing insects found in the house. I pick them up in a piece of Kleenex and put them outside. I'm pleased to see spiders, scorpions and even hornets go on with their lives. I have a few large variety roaches coming to visit now and then. I see them as my ancient friends and give them the benefit of fresh air. I'd like to think these kooky ways have something to do with respect for life as a part of spiritual practice.

In the late eighties and early nineties, I was moving toward a spirituality of the ordinary, the human, the earthly. The deaths of two people and a beloved dog toward the end of this period sum up these tendencies. The passing of special people has a way of drawing one back to essentials in life's brief sojourn. My uncle John, "*Barba Gianni*," died in his sleep after a long period of declining health and heart disease. It came as a shock to me and my brother George who had taken good care of him. Neighbors had seen John on the street the day before. Yet it was a merciful way for him to go. He was a simple man, an old bachelor who would have hated loss of independence and the indignities of the modern death technology with its strange places, people, and machines. Death has a way of giving us a tableau of a person's fundamental spirit. There was his crusty, angry, contrarian side. There was a lifetime of struggle with the remnants of his nervous breakdown as a soldier. But he never lost his inner child and his unique sense of humor. People thought of him as childlike.

Yet Uncle John bonded with me in a special way. For all his "craziness," he was probably the sanest person in the family. He was able to connect on a level of caring and humor. He brought his own religion about as far down as it could come to earth. Rejecting the parish church, which was partially responsible for his scruples, he set up his own chapel in a backyard chicken coop, a remnant of our "Victory Garden" during the war. I still have a plastic statuette from this shrine. He knew how to satirize the pompousness of the church, which, he thought, disregarded him in old age, seeing him as a person of no account. His satire created a kind of personal kabuki. For example, he would vocalize and act out the sound of the chain hitting the side of an incense container as a priest swung it: "Dominus, Sancta Pachinka, Pachinka, Pacha." Then he would add for good measure: "John Mangini, for your sins you are condemned to hell for all eternity."

He was specially devoted to the Ohlone burial grounds in Emeryville near the San Francisco Bay. He would make regular pilgrimages there. Stray cats clustered around him. The lost were comforting the lost. Oddly enough, of all the adults in my childhood, this childlike man became the most capable of an adult relationship. He wasn't judgmental or loaded with expectations. With him, you got what you saw, and he reciprocated by viewing you at a more basic level. He was probably the holiest of us all.

Animals have come to be spiritually important to me. Maybe this is heightened by not having children of my own. In 1995, we put down my standard poodle, Jenny, after thirteen years as my constant companion. In some ways, her relation to me was akin to Uncle John's. She was direct, accepting, living in the present and close to natural rhythms. On the day of her death, my Taoist meditation was on non-duality, on not being separate from nature and from this dog. I wrote in my journal: "She will live with me as long as I can remember. As we were about to get into my truck, she sat in the driveway looking back at the house and garden for a long moment. Before the vet administered the injection, I held her head, kissed her, thanked her for our life together, and told her that I loved her. She looked at me the whole time. We had a similar experience more recently with our second standard, Rhainy. After many years of exuberant living and caring, she died surrounded by Peggy and me and a vet who cared for her. I think she knew that her time had come. Like Jenny, she made a final tour of the house and garden, looked long at the river, and as I said in a memento note, taught us how to die.

In some ways, Anselm Atkins was the opposite of Uncle John. Anselm, as I noted earlier, was a distinguished mind. He held a doctorate from the Institute of Liberal Arts at Emory. He had been a Trappist monk and priest in Conyers, Georgia and a well-published author. He also became a very fine stained glass artist. Anselm rejected organized religion and its doctrines. He saw himself as a humanist and naturalist. His saint became Darwin. I contrast him to my Uncle John, but, in important ways, they were similar.

Anselm had a childlike sweetness and humor about him that was thoroughly inviting. He expressed this comedy side in many published cartoons in Catholic magazines during his Trappist years. He published articles in *The Humanist* about his reasons for denying the validity of religion. Had he lived longer, he would have fit into the current chorus of atheists in the popular press. But he had more gentleness and humility about him. His arguments were prompted by philosophical and scientific inquiry, not by personal problems with the church. I remember our conversations over beer in the kitchen of his unique house. We talked about evolution and religion as well as homier topics like his bicycle tours across Georgia and his favorite professional football teams. But for Anselm, the more he studied the science of nature, the more he abandoned the case for religion. Our disagreements never altered our respect for each other and our enjoyment of being with a friend. I may be pushing it a bit, but his prominently displayed stained glass piece in our home of two intertwined but happy snakes might represent our duality. We had both gone from sky religion to earth awareness, but with different outcomes.

Not long before he died of cancer, I wrote a letter of response to his article in *The Humanist* where he described his journey into naturalist atheism. I'd like to cite a section of it to close this chapter because it sums up my similar but different intellectual bent. In an odd way, I was build-ing on his own namesake, St. Anselm, who saw his personal journey as *fides quaerens intellectum*, faith seeking understanding:

"What I say is not a refutation of your argument. There is no re-futing it if one accepts your presuppositions. Your argument is like a beautiful onion in a hermetically sealed jar. You peel back one bright, eye-stinging layer after another. You want to disabuse us of bad thinking. You want us to live courageously, to accept the limits of our finitude and not build false castles."

"Let me lay out a few premises of my own. I'm convinced of natural evolution. I think all energy is ultimately unitary. That may be a way of saying that there are not souls hiding in bodies, waiting to make their escape. I don't know what happens after death. It may be extinction of consciousness and a return to the cosmic energy pool. Or it may be something else, some entry into a new dimension of awareness. I don't believe in special interventions by God on the part of humans. Jenny (my poodle) was better than most of us anyway. Why would a smart God be so dumb as to favor us alone. After many years of reflection, I have demythologized Christian and other religious stories. I see these narratives as still developing products of the human imagination grap-pling with life and death. These are symbol and cult systems forged out of millennia of human experience. They are tremendously interesting for what they are as the spirit dimension of the human quest. I also find many aspects of these religions helpful for a seeker on the spiritual path. I don't think we should cut off the possibilities of transcendent experience with tightly sealed arguments that seem scientific, but in the end are non-scientific because they foreclose different options in an a-priori way."

I realize the danger of self-justification in quoting from my letter, but since this is my memoir, I might look more benignly on the effort as an attempt at self-understanding.

I see two motions in this time of my life. One is the move to define myself by a cluster of adjectives as a metaphorical, Arian, agnostic, cosmopolitan (the Eastern influences that I will expand on in the next chapter) Catholic Christian. I suspect all these labels, although I use them, *faut de mieux.* These monikers are to some extent true of me. Yet, as the Buddha would say, they are only concepts. The real entity is my complex, embodied person with tenuous ideas and conflicted feelings. The second motion of this period may help explain the adjectives in a more realistic way. Specific experiences that helped define my inner spirit.

Even though I chose a certain career path, much of it just happened to me. I became a professor of religion because certain options opened up and I followed them. I probably would not have been as influenced by Asian wisdom had I not landed at Emory where such traditions were highly prized. After a lifetime of study, religious words take on special meaning. But these intellectual categories don't exist in a vacuum. They, too, are shaped by the concrete experiences of what was going on in my marital and social life (I met these specific women and made these particular friends) as well as in national and worldwide happenings. The work of grace comes through all that.

1991: GENE AND PEGGY AT CITY HALL IN ATHENS, GEORGIA

9

Staying Open to Inner Voices

In a room where people unanimously maintain a conspiracy of silence,
one word of truth sounds like a pistol shot.

—Czesław Miłosz

As I begin this chapter, I'm sitting in a Starbucks on Fisherman's Wharf surrounded by young people focused on their sweetened drinks. I don't think they like the taste of coffee just yet. At seventy-seven I think about my own youth in San Francisco. I entered high school here, and then became a Jesuit and eventually left the order from this town. Now I'm aware of being an elder. I've written books about getting older, but now I'm doing my lab, as it were. Throughout this memoir, I've been trying to decipher inner changes. For the last decade especially, most things register against the backdrop of aging. This isn't a sad condition because my health is good, I'm blessed with Peggy and other friends as well as interesting things to do. Unlike my father, I'm not the proverbial pensioner sitting on a bench in Oakland's Mosswood Park with other oldsters watching the world go by. I've been very engaged in things. That's part of the problem as I look ahead. I may be ignoring key aspects of my own aging. I can see this as I review my journals for recent years. A major polarity shows up between doing and being, between my active agenda and how best to embrace a contemplative life.

André Hayen, whom I mentioned earlier, gives us a clue for this question. He wrote an essay about his leaving the order in his seventies to marry. He talks about responding to an inner calling, an *intention profonde* that he tried to honor throughout his life. He discusses moving from a bourgeois, idealized version of life to immersion in bodily love and being for others. There was no need to convert others, he thought, but to help them find a wisdom already within themselves, that is, their *intention profonde*. This search led to his *déviance*, his shocking late departure from a respected role in the order. But it was also a deviance from externalized religion to life in his own body. In a cruder example from Thich Nhat Hanh, it was something like letting the mud settle to see clear water. So I want to keep asking the question about my own *intention profonde*. How might I best let it speak from and to me? How might it become clearer to me amid the continuing complexities of older age?

As I approached formal retirement, the Religion Department sponsored the publication of a small festschrift in my honor, called *Selving*. The title comes from the Jesuit poet, Gerald Manley Hopkins:

> As kingfishers catch fire, dragonflies draw flame;
> As tumbled over rim in roundy wells
> Stones ring; like each tucked string tells, each hung bell's
> Bow swung finds tongue to fling out broad its name;
> Each mortal thing does one thing and the same:
> Deals out that being indoors each one dwells;
> Selves—goes itself; myself it speaks and spells,
> Crying What I do is me: for that I came.
> —"AS KINGFISHERS CATCH FIRE"

So, too, the theme of this memoir derives from Hopkins's idea of the self ever becoming in the concreteness of life. It's a dynamic notion that turns inward for ultimate guidance rather than outward. It reflects one of my favorite lines in the Gnostic Gospel of Thomas: "He who brings out what is within will be saved." Many early Christians lived by such gospels before they were suppressed by the hierarchy in the third century for a more externalized version of Christianity, one easier to keep under clerical control.

In *Selving*, my Jesuit classmate Jim Torrens underscores our differences when he notes how our paths diverged, his road one of loyalty, mine one of criticism. Actually both paths are needed for creativity. A person can pursue his inner vision while continuing in the formal structures of the church. But there is also something in the fundamental chemistry of the Society of Jesus, as intuited by Hopkins and acknowledged by Ignatius, that in the end, one is called to follow the inward consolations of the Holy Spirit. This sometimes leads to a spiritual unruliness that continues to get Jesuits in trouble with a rule-bound

Vatican. It is still another instance of following André Hayen's search for *intention profonde*.

As I approached retirement, I brought together a group of faculty from different parts of the university to explore the idea of an Emeritus College. This new unit at Emory would continue to connect retired faculty to one another and to the mission of the university. It was another experiment in aging. Of course, we do these things partially for ourselves. I didn't want to cut ties to colleagues with whom I had spent a major part of my adult life. After a little probing, it was clear that many other retiring faculty felt the same way. We benefit from the insights and friendships of our fellows in the many programs of the Emeritus College. We could also make new contributions to the university and the wider community. A fellow theologian, Provost Rebecca Chopp, was open to this vision and willing to provide a pilot budget for two years.

A few successful retirement organizations, especially in California schools, acted as models. Yet the project at Emory was something of a creation from nothing. However, I didn't feel like the Creator of Genesis as I scrounged for office equipment among remnants of furniture in the old Georgia Regional Mental Health Center, newly purchased by Emory. It is the nature of grace to come unexpectedly. This came in the person of my administrative assistant, Rhonda Dubin, who had the right combination of charism and discipline to help make the venture work. The Emeritus College sponsored a full schedule of events from an art gallery for faculty exhibitions to monthly breakfast and lunch discussions to special receptions and lectures. The main personal benefit as director has been new friendships among retirees across the university from arts and sciences to the health fields. It allowed physicians to talk with sociologists and business school people to discuss with artists.

But as Peggy reminds me, it was also a way to retire while not retiring. What looked like being rehired for a part time job grew into more than that at Emory and elsewhere. I participated in starting a national group, the Association of Retirement Organizations in Higher Education. The original impetus for AROHE came from the University of Southern California under the leadership of the late Professor Paul Hadley. I became its second president in 2005. It was inspiring to work with colleagues around the country as well as Canada. We helped incipient emeritus groups with the experiences of established organizations and we shared best practices among schools. Universities showed growing interest in enhancing the life of retirees and fostering their value to institutions and to one another.

These involvements brought up old questions. Am I still too addicted to the culture of striving? When I left the nest on 42nd and Market in Oakland at eighteen, had I learned only one way to fly? Was I still a driven workaholic after all the spiritual lessons? Well, yes and no. The Promethean push was still there. We were taught to bring back the life-giving fire. And work of some kind benefits the aging process. That theme is in all my books on growing older. Emeritus College turned out to be a legacy for colleagues and a benefit to me.

Yet my journals during this period show longings for silence, solitude and contemplation. I talk about wanting soul work to be foremost in all my projects. One day the pendulum on my antique, wind-up clock stopped during a meditation. It made me think of how hard it was to halt the rush of time and its tasks. The clock was calling me to rest quietly in this moment while listening gently to the parade of my desires. I had started to meditate on Zen teacher Joko Beck's suggestion of letting go of excessive desires with their cacophony of "what ifs" to find peace in my present reality. I wanted to be more like Master Dogen alive to the particular in the now, to this frog plopping in this water.

What was at the heart of this polarity between my passion for work and my hope for a deeper contemplative life? The easy answer is to rely on what I said earlier about the benefits of work and the value of keeping a good balance between the active and the contemplative. The Jesuit ideal is to be a *contemplativus in actione*. But that's the teacher in me tying a nice bow around a just-given lecture. If I seek an answer closer to my gut feelings and fears, my quest for the contemplative is to learn how to die well, how to cope with anxieties about my own mortality. Teilhard's words keep coming back: *il faut finir bien*. To some this may seem morbid, but it really isn't. One of our annual programs in Emeritus College concerned "Advance Directives," that is, how to prepare loved ones for our passing by getting one's house in order.

Yet these good ideas about living wills and powers of attorney look at death from the outside. My hope for a fuller contemplative life has to do with inner advance directives on my own death. As I've said to numerous classes on death and dying, to really be at peace with my dying will help me live more fully in the remaining time. I don't agree with the poet's injunction to "rage, rage against the dying of the light . . ." I want to "go gentle into that good night." I want to accept the evolutionary imperative (as my unconsciously Darwinian grandmother used to say in her Genoese dialect, *se gemmu da moui,* we have to die) as an event of grace.

In recent years, two deaths of lifelong Jesuit friends bring home these points. One was the sudden passing of Ed Malatesta, a member of my novice class of 1948. He had fallen sick while traveling in Asia not long after undergoing major prostate surgery. When Jim Torrens told me of his death, I said that Ed needed a wife to scream at him not to take long plane trips so soon after surgery, given his particular pulmonary weaknesses. In an odd way, I was indirectly lecturing the Jesuits on the values of a married religious order. Peggy would have sat on my head to keep me from such travel in those circumstances. But, of course, I felt Ed's loss. Peggy and I had visited him in convalescence only months before.

Malatesta and I admired each other but we were not easy friends. He was a very committed man. I used to call him *immensa voluntas,* massive willpower. He accomplished much, especially in organizing the Ricci Institute at USF for historical studies of Jesuits in China. He criticized me for leaving the order. It took a long time for that fissure to heal. Part of his reaction flowed from his own fervent dedication to the Society and the church.

Paul Belcher's death was even more shocking, since he died accidentally when a heavy gate at his parish crashed down on him. My friendship with Paul was more of a connatural happening, a delight in being with one another whether in or out of the order. He wore his high office of Provincial lightly. He was very accessible and fun to be with in any circumstance. In 1963 we delivered a VW Bug to Denver, going on by bus to Milwaukee to study German, and then on again by bus to New York for graduate study. I remember telling him that as a sociologist he needed to study the culture of Greyhound stations. We walked annually in Golden Gate Park to discuss the church and world. He met my wives with kindness and good spirits. Yet both of these deaths brought home the reality of my own passing. Neither man got his prayers answered according to the litany that Jesuits recited: "From a sudden and unforeseen death, deliver us, O Lord." But I'm being too literal about this. Ed and Paul were ready in their own ways.

Peggy and I experienced a much longer dying process with her mother, Frances, whose slow decline from Alzheimer's covered a decade.

We faced difficult decisions about keeping her at home or placing her in an institution. A remarkably fine facility, Presbyterian Village, took Frances first into assisted living and eventually into their nursing home. As the care-giving daughter, Peggy had to work through her feelings about removing her mother from our home. As we built our new house, it was always a poignant scene with her mother asking when she could come home. Her question would come back to me when I walked into the lovely suite prepared for the woman who would never see it. Professional advice and the experience of friends who kept an Alzheimer's patient at home convinced us that it would be better for Frances and for us to place her in Presbyterian Village. She would get better care and have more social stimulation. Peggy, while still working at the University of Georgia, was very solicitous about Frances, checking frequently with her care-givers. We visited regularly. Watching Peggy handle the situation, while going through the strain of a lawsuit against the university (which she won after three years), made me realize that I had, indeed, married well. Here was a loving person who would know when to pull the plug.

Frances became a spiritual teacher in her declining years. Despite her growing limitations, she displayed her signature brand of gruff humor. The staff loved her spunk. "The hell you say I need a bath," she would say. On other occasions she would turn and tell her caregivers that she really loved them. The staff appreciated that indomitable spark of humanity in trying times. As the illness progressed, she reverted to her core spirit from childhood. There in old age was the skeptical, playful tomboy who enjoyed doing pranks and not taking too seriously her observant Baptist parents. I don't want to minimize the tragedy of the disease, but Frances gave me lessons on how to meet the final adversity. Since she couldn't remember what was said a few minutes earlier, she reminded me about the importance of living in the moment. Peggy read to her and I did sketches of her. She would get us laughing with "Dear God, do I look that bad?" Again, she was the lovable contrarian, who would interrupt us with: "You know, I really love you two." She made a few words go a long way.

I've made a lot in this memoir of moving from the abstract to the concrete, from sky to earth, from concepts to the body. Frances's long bout with Alzheimer's taught me that lesson. More recently, I took on some of the care of my longtime, ex-Jesuit friend, Tom Till, also a victim of the same disease. I had him examined for the illness at Emory's hospital, and helped him move into a special care facility in Chattanooga. His wife, Gerri, who was dying of cancer during Tom's decline, was able to call on an old convent friend to take on close oversight and befriending of Tom in his last years.

Barbara Gale, my therapeutic masseuse in Athens, Georgia, introduced me to another body-spirit connection. In truculent male fashion, I resisted getting a massage when Peggy suggested I go. It just didn't seem manly, though I wouldn't say that to Peggy, of course. That I was too busy with the back and forth between Athens and Atlanta made a better excuse. But once I tried it, I became an easy convert. The experience depends partially on the rapport between physical therapist and client. I'm sure that the bodily benefit of the massage would obtain with any capable practitioner. But Barbara brought her own spiritual experiences to the table, as it were.

She and her husband, a professor and therapist, both from Jewish backgrounds, are very open to wisdom experiences from other traditions. They attend retreats on yoga and other spiritual practices. What's spiritual about massage? I'd say that it's an experience of sensual mysticism in the moment. By mysticism here I mean a unitive experience of body, mind and feelings. It is at once a receiving and a giving, a way of being with another person for a meditative hour without words, for the most part. Is it sensual? Of course. Is it erotic? I would say yes, while correcting the misuse of that word in our overly sexualized culture. Have I fallen in love with Barbara? That, too, if I can fall back on my conviction that love is not a zero-sum game. Maybe the best way for me to explain this phenomenon is to cite a poem I wrote for Barbara's fiftieth birthday:

> "Wordless therapy hour
> like surf caressing wet sand . . .
> Time stops and we sink heavy through pillows into now.
> If eyes are mirrors of the soul,
> Pressing, kneading, gliding hands
> open soul to soul.
> Distances fade, anticipations cease;
> Male and female chi links beyond sex.
> Asklepios smiles and the Lark descends . . .
> This is my body, this is my blood."

The eucharistic reference in the last line connects with what I said earlier about holy communion as an experience in tangible life. I re-

ferred to my cousin Luisa's open table as a eucharistic rite. Here it is a
kind of soul food, an inner bread kneaded by hand. Again, it reminds me
of Teilhard's "The Mass on the World." The priest moves from church to
a natural altar. The Greek for Eucharist, moreover, denotes thanksgiving,
gratefulness. The massage always ends with a sincere thank-you and a
hug on the way out.

In the fall of 2000, I was invited to teach a course in world religions
at John Cabot University in Rome. I rented a room from a retired Italian
professor of English, Carlo Cesarini, just a few blocks from St. Peter's
Square. It was also the Holy Year with a constant stream of tourists and
pilgrims heading for the Eternal City. On my early morning walks up
the Janiculum hill, I took a shortcut through the new parking terminal
for buses. Every day I saw busloads of faithful with colorful banners and
special tee shirts marching toward St. Peter's. That I was headed in the
opposite direction may have symbolized our differences. I had nothing
against pilgrimages to the Pope. I wasn't a true anti-clerical. Part of my
morning hike was to stop in the quaint little church of Sant'Onofrio for
meditation. As I sat in the empty church, I thought about Pope Pius IX,
Pio Nono, the reactionary who restored this building in the nineteenth
century. Here I was helping myself to the good graces of Pio Nono, who,
had he been present, would have chased me from the premises as a rav-
ing heretic. I might even have ended up in a rough, horse-drawn car-
riage that used to pass down the street where I lodged on its way to meet
the papal executioner. I thought of that, too, as I did yoga on the balcony
overlooking that road.

Another somber figure hovering over me in Sant'Onofrio, was Pius
X in an epic-size painting. He had been the hammer of Catholic mod-
ernists, people of my bent, at the turn of the twentieth century. In the
mural his right hand was raised in benediction. I imagined a hatchet in
it. But the legendary wall paintings of Onofrio himself and his exploits
in the outside cloister calmed me. Wild beasts refused to eat him. They
sat at his feet and brought him food. Now, there's my kind of saint. So
despite Pius IX and X, I felt that the lions would do as much for me if I
invoked Onofrio. I saw here something of the richness of the Catholic
tradition. In one small church, there were those who would do me in
as well as the Onofrio type who would invite me into his cave, have me
sit by the tiger and pour me a glass of Chianti. Notice here, too, the
difference between sky and earth religion. There were the richly-robed

popes protecting what they thought was unchangeable orthodoxy. In the cloister, Onofrio mostly in the buff, hadn't seen a barber in years. His mythology was closer to earth religion than theirs.

My morning walks on the Janiculum characterized my relationship with the church. I absorbed the mythopoetic symbolism of Onofrio, while I observed two popes locked into Catholic fundamentalism. I was sitting under Pius X's "hatchet" musing about how I could make Buddhism and Taoism intelligible to thirty students later that day at the college in the Trastevere district. This tableau in Sant'Onofrio isn't meant to depreciate religious believers. Rather it expresses a different frame of reference that divides not only Catholicism, but other churches and religious institutions. A frame of reference can be called a paradigm, as Marcus Borg explains in reference to the New Testament in his book *Jesus*. The paradigm about religion in the minds of those two popes and perhaps the majority of the pilgrims walking to St. Peter's is pre-Copernican. pre-scientific, pre-Enlightenment. This large body of religious people are not opposed to modern science as it manifests itself in technological advances. Religious pre-Copernicans are perfectly contemporary when they drive their cars, use computers, fly in airplanes and expect the latest medical treatments. But in matters of religion they think and find comfort in pre-Enlightenment ways.

A few characteristics of this paradigm are literal interpretations of Scripture, fixed concepts of doctrine, and resistance to change in the church. The pre-Copernican world was one of perceived stability. The earth and its people were at the center of God's universe. Everything revolved around them. Priests pronounced doctrines from this perspective. This worldview lends itself to maximizing one's own religion as the true understanding of the universe story. It is resistant to ecumenism. It insists on certainty and conformity. For pre-Copernicans agnosticism is tantamount to atheism.

For such believers metaphorical ways of interpreting Scripture or doctrine, hallmarks of post-Copernicans, betray the past and its once-and-for-all revelation. (Actually, metaphorical understandings of many New Testament passages give more accurate understandings of their real meaning.) To see theology as mythic, for these people, amounts to calling it falsehood. The pre-Copernican mentality also understands authority in the church as coming from above. The divinely anointed status of pope and bishop is fixed from on high, just as that of king or emperor was in the past. It becomes extremely hard to introduce change in these hierarchical systems, because they are seen as willed by God. They are as permanent as the steady state firmament that was once thought to revolve around us. As long as enough people parade to St. Peter's with this mind-set, consciously or unconsciously, the easier it is for authorities to preserve their niches of power.

Living in Rome during the Holy Year of 2000 helped me size up my spiritual direction. I could appreciate in a more tangible way certain values of the Catholic tradition. Despite its many sins over the centuries, the church could still tap into deep currents of religious motivation and action for human welfare. It could still open a way toward transcendent experience. I rebelled against the portrait of the founder of Opus Dei, Josemaría Escrivá de Balaguer hanging in front of St. Peter's in lieu of his canonization. Opus Dei is a very conservative organization, combining political involvements with a severe, authoritarian ethos. Yet I remembered that Angelo Roncalli, Pope John XXIII, a modern reformist saint, was buried in St. Peter's crypt. The church still incorporated the best of its teachings in the lives of individuals and groups who cared about humanity and the planet. I was reminded that Catholicism was a baggy pants operation. Or in the sentiments of James Joyce, here comes everybody.

One afternoon coming back from teaching, I ran into Cardinal Josef Ratzinger standing alone in front of his Palace of the Holy Office. Dressed in ordinary black clerical garb, he looked like any other priest. He was waiting for a ride to dinner. We chatted amiably for a while and then went our ways. Little did I know then that he would become Benedict XVI. I've thought about that chance meeting a number of times. He stood for many things that I, as a theologian, would criticize. His officially non-democratic ways were repugnant to me. He was called "God's rottweiler," for condemning liberal theologians. He and his successors at the Congregation for the Defense of the Faith tried to suppress Catholic luminaries like Anthony de Mello and Hans Küng; they also launched the recent inquisition of American Catholic nuns. Ratzinger encapsulated much of what I saw as obstacles to needed reform, and he still does. Yet in the declining light of that late fall afternoon, we were two people who recognized the humanity of the other, each in very different but concrete ways trying to live gospel values.

The same Roman sojourn highlighted what I didn't like about the church. There was too much emphasis on the glorification of hierarchy, on the pope as a sacral figure. The sacred was still too far removed from the ordinary, from the everyday life of people. The rites in St. Peter's Square emphasized this distance. In email letters from Rome to friends, I enjoyed poking fun at some of the folderol surrounding the Holy Year. The "popemobile" tours of John Paul II through the crowds could be charitably interpreted as the desire of the Pope to get close to the faithful. But to me, these descents into the masses were little better than Pope Pius XII of my earlier years being carried around on a *sedia gestatoria*, the throne borne on the shoulders of papal householders. I knew that it was part of ecclesiastical show biz and not to be taken too seriously. But I also thought about George Washington who resisted attempts to make him an American king. My brother thought I was Catholic-bashing in these postings. Others seemed to enjoy the letters.

During this time, I began writing a light novella, "Jesus in Jeans, Buddha on a Motor Scooter." I imagined meeting Jesus at the Bar Dante on the Janiculum hill. He had returned as an information officer at Leonardo Da Vinci airport, and was living with a girlfriend, Magda, who mentored disabled children. They had a close friend, a rotund Asian, Biko, who worked at the Vatican post office and tore around Rome on a bright saffron *motorino*. This was a strange Second Coming, far less ominous than Yeats's somber figure slouching toward Bethlehem. But Jesus in jeans presented an earthly spirit in contrast to the sky religion hovering over the Vatican. I had Jesus carrying a full laundry sack across St. Peter's Square during a major papal appearance. I asked him what he thought of it all. He gave me a balanced but unenthusiastic response. I told him about my meeting with Cardinal Ratzinger. Jesus leaned over to whisper that His Eminence, too, put his pants on one leg at a time. I asked him for a gospel reference. He said he was too busy just now, as Magda was waiting for him at the laundromat off *Piazza Risorgimento*. He left me thinking that the new *risorgimento* of spirit would come from earthlings not hierarchs.

Jesus and Buddha as buddies or brothers may seem too casual a statement. It risks lessening the dignity due to these great wisdom teachers. And "being brothers" doesn't deny differences between them. But the thrust of "Jesus in Jeans" points to ways that such spiritual traditions can find new common ground. This will be by rubbing shoulders in mutual tasks and friendships. Jesus could have used a ride to the laundromat on Buddha's motor scooter.

In recent years, I've also pursued this topic of mixing spiritual heritages by interviewing many religion teachers who have moved toward the East in their personal spiritual journeys. These men and women are able to integrate for themselves the insights of various traditions. There is still strong opposition in conservative quarters to what is seen as "cafeteria spirituality," the selective choosing of ideas and practices to one's liking. It is derided as superficiality and disloyalty to certain beliefs. It's hard to predict the future of these trans-traditional movements. What might they look like a century from now? But Teilhard de Chardin's theme of the convergence of minds across the planet should increase with our new technologies for communication.

My study (with Peter McDonough) of contemporary American Jesuits and former Jesuits (*Passionate Uncertainty: Inside the American Jesuits*) underscores such ecumenical engagements. A leading figure in this movement was Anthony de Mello, SJ, whose books and retreats incorporated themes from Hinduism and Buddhism. The study and practice of such traditions, especially Buddhism and Taoism, have strongly influenced me. As a Hindu colleague at Emory reminds me, Buddhism was originally an Indian religion that carries forward many aspects of its Hindu sources. I am also indebted to the Sufi mystical traditions of Rumi and Kabir. I am constantly struck by similarities among Eastern contemplatives and the mystical expressions of Catherine of Siena and Teresa of Avila. They all describe an experience of union with God or the transcendent through the natural world and human interactions. I realize that my knowledge of Eastern traditions is filtered through a Western screen. We in the West have chosen to focus on the psycho-spiritual and meditative aspects of these heritages rather than on their ritual, institutional and more esoteric dimensions. We have been selective consumers of these religions.

What I appreciate most about Eastern religious wisdom is its focus on inwardness. It underscores the subtle ways by which our thoughts and desires impede enlightenment or a life of deeper awareness. Reflective practices help us to see how excessive desires lead to ignorance and negative attitudes of greed, hatred and violence. These poisons in turn destroy the spirit of compassion and harm social life. I recognize that this nexus between one's inner life and its outward expression is also present in Western spirituality and mysticism. Unfortunately, the contemplative life has not been stressed as central in the more externalized practices of Western religion. It took discovery of the East to bring me back to appreciation of my own Western mystical tradition.

Eastern traditions also free one from the literal fixity of belief systems. For a long time Christian beliefs about God, Jesus, and the Bible were set in historical-literal molds rather than understood according to figurative interpretations. Authority figures insisted on acceptance of certain beliefs for salvation. Eastern religions have had their own authority problems in terms of spiritual teachers who could abuse their disciples by demanding slavish obedience. But the Buddha's last words, "Be a lamp unto yourself," acted as a remedy against such abuse. I respect religious beliefs about God, for example, as imaginative, metaphorical projects that can illuminate and inspire. But too often teachers present them in absolute, literal ways that denigrate religion in the eyes of reflective people. Much of the contemporary atheistic attack on religion aims at such literal supernaturalism.

Taoism really speaks to me. It underscores nature as a guide toward the Tao, that mysterious source pervading the world of which we are a part. It may be the ancient spiritual movement most removed from sky religion. Chinese landscape paintings as well as the *Tao Te Ching* immerse us in scenes of earth. Lao Tse's teaching about not-knowing pulls us away from our satisfaction with concepts, especially in the spiritual realm. In this sense, it echoes the medieval Christian classic, *The Cloud of Unknowing*. When we become convinced of how little we know, we drop our conceptual blockages to experiencing the divine or the Tao in the world. Taoist teaching of non-doing acts as a balance to my workaholic proclivities. Yet this is not an invitation to passivity. It means doing non-doing, that is, acting in the world sensitive to how things are and without attachment to my desired outcomes. It adds a distinctive layer of understanding to the Jesuit motto of being a contemplative in action. I fail often in reaching such high levels of mindfulness. But these ideals should not make us feel guilty for not attaining them. That would be to set a false desired outcome. Rather the goal of doing non-doing gently prods us to walk more compassionately on the earth.

Yet Catholic teachers writing about "going East" have had a hard time with authorities. Thomas Merton (*Zen and the Birds of Appetite*) was a precursor for me. He seemed to be moving closer to Eastern spiritual-

ity when he died in Bangkok at a conference on such inter-religious topics. He appears to have operated under the Vatican radar, which was still
relatively quiet in the wake of Vatican II. But the Vatican Congregation
for the Doctrine of the Faith criticized perceived errors of de Mello.
The CDF censured his moderate colleague at the Gregorian University,
Jacques Dupuis, for his positions on dialogue with Eastern religions.
Without going into details, my objection to these Vatican ways is not a
rejection of honest disagreement. It is rather the bureaucratic, secretive,
and authoritarian mode of condemnation. This does not encourage open
discussion of issues among peers. It does not indulge sufficiently in Lao
Tse's "not-knowing." Benedict XVI has more recently raised obstacles to
ecumenism among Christians by reaffirming the doctrine of the one,
true church while other Christian bodies (the Orthodox excepted) are
seen as lesser churches.

But Rome's negative reactions may actually prove the strength of
ecumenical ventures in recent decades. The rebuffs from official sources
may be fingers in the dike of an irrepressible wave. Of course, the future is always unpredictable. And today's globalization may not of itself
produce a universalizing spirit. Combative Catholics and Protestants
in northern Ireland lived in close proximity as have Sunnis and Shia
in Iraq. Beyond physical nearness, it will take an attitude of dialogue,
tolerance and curiosity about the beliefs of others, and most importantly, respect for the person of the neighbor. The element of curiosity
brings up a memory of my interview in Claremont, California with John
Coleman Bennett near the end of his life. This Protestant ethicist and
former president of Union Theological Seminary, expressed a special
warmth toward me in my student days at Union. He said that a major
disappointment about dying was the challenge to his spirit of curiosity.
"I'd love to know how things will turn out," he said. We can only guess at
the prospects of ecumenism among and within world religions in light
of globalization. But communication technologies offer new hope for
such creative dialogue.

My interviews among Jesuits and former Jesuits for *Passionate
Uncertainty* also opened up issues concerning sexuality and celibacy.
The number of American Jesuits had declined by more than half over a
forty year period. This in itself is an astounding statistic, especially since
there were no outward pressures on the order from potentates as in the
eighteenth century. Vatican II opened up radical reassessments of the

celibate life. This memoir attests to my personal journey in dealing with sexuality after twenty years as a celibate. After the council the perennial links between celibacy and ministry were broken. The arguments of a millennium joining priesthood to the celibate life became unconvincing for many. There is no need here to further rehearse the rationale that brought about this watershed era in the church. An extensive library now exists to explain the transformation. Not only celibacy was called into question. Catholic teaching on sexuality in general with its largely negative and dualistic tenets about body and soul were disintegrating. Changed attitudes about birth control among Catholics bear evidence of this. My novella "Jesus in Jeans" describes a non-clerical Jesus who lives with his girlfriend.

The close link between celibacy and priestly ministry struck me as I watched the proceedings of the last Jesuit General Congregation in Rome. The Society of Jesus elected a progressive new general superior and set forth some admirable goals for the order. But the Society's worldwide membership has dropped by more than half since Vatican II. Yet everyone seems content to walk around the unseen eight hundred pound gorilla of celibacy in the center of the room. One might well argue that with Pope Benedict XVI nearby, there was no way of exploring the sexual arrangement of priestly life. But it doesn't take much imagination to conclude that the Catholic priesthood would attract many more recruits by unchaining ministry from celibacy. This larger pool of candidates would also improve the quality of applicants. More high caliber men and women would take up a priestly role in the church in general and religious orders in particular. The small number of annual novices entering the Society today represent not only a quantitative but also a qualitative decline. During my twenty years in the order, there was a much larger core of highly talented people than today. Such developments, including women priests, would require changes in the constitutions of orders. But these celibate institutions are not essential to Christianity. The need for this change seems so clear to me that I find it flying in the face of common sense to deny it.

In our study of American Jesuits, I was surprised at how gay the order had become. Among those under fifty, the proportions rose to 50 percent and more, as noted by Jesuits themselves. But beyond the numbers, an overt homosexual lifestyle had developed. During my years in the Society, we were aware of gay companions, but a strong "don't ask, don't tell" policy prevailed. The church had long condemned homosexuality as intrinsically disordered and unnatural. Now with the gay liberation movement launched in the wider culture, homosexuals in the order also wanted to be free to live in less hidden ways. As the overall numbers of Jesuits dropped, many of whom wanted to marry, the gay contingent became more prominent. Of course, gays also left during the exodus of the sixties and seventies. But an all-male order provided a more congenial environment for homosexuals who could continue their vocations as religious ministers while cultivating satisfying friendships with men.

Since the child abuse controversy in recent years, gay clerics have had to assume a lower profile. Although the majority of child abusers in society are heterosexuals, the official church focused blame on gay clergy. The main point I want to make on the gay issue concerns the link between homosexuality and a celibate clerical culture. The generally respected world of celibate priests (until the child abuse storm) was an ideal place for homosexual Catholic men inclined to ministry to live and thrive. This is not meant as an argument against gays in the priesthood. Most of these men have served the church well for centuries. But the new discussion brings up a complex question. How wise is it, pastorally speaking, for the church to have a majority gay clergy? The Vatican has established new guidelines for seminarians as a way of preventing some gays from entering the priesthood. But it is highly questionable whether these procedures will work in Western culture where the gay lifestyle is largely accepted.

The gay issue, while significant in itself, points to a more important subject. What is the meaning of human sexuality? Official Catholic responses have evolved in a culture of celibacy. The institutional core of the church, the final arbiter of sexual interpretations, is the celibate hierarchy. Nearly all Catholic teachings on sex emanate from celibate leaders. The official mindset on sexuality from birth control to the ordination of women radiates from top level celibates. The struggle to preserve celibacy can lead to strange views about chastity for men and women. An example would be official teaching about masturbation that condemns a practice that modern psychology finds normal. The opposition to women's ordination has both political and sexual dimensions. Women priests and bishops represent a threat to the celibate ruling group on two levels, that of defending purity, as understood by Rome, and that of sharing power.

One evening in 1994, as I mentioned earlier, Peggy and I were relaxing in a *pensione* near the Palazzo Doria Pamphili in Rome after a long day of sightseeing in the summer heat. Pope John Paul had just issued a proclamation against the ordination of women. He also ordered Catholics not to discuss the issue since the answer was absolutely clear to him that such a move was impossible in light of tradition. When leaders demand silence in this way, one wonders how secure they are in their own views. Peggy saw it as another power move to preserve the status quo. The anatomical arguments invoking the will of God were less than convincing. Church leaders routinely revert to God's will to justify arrangements that benefit them. The rationale came down to this: Jesus was male; therefore, women did not have the correct organs for ordination to the priesthood. Strong evidence exists that there were women priests in the early church (Karen Torjesen, *When Women Were Priests*) and even women bishops. It is also clear that there were married priests in the West until the Middle Ages.

The arguments against a married leadership rest on a long history of mandatory celibacy since the twelfth century. As I intimated above when discussing the Jesuit General Congregation, there is little hope of serious structural reform in Catholicism without changing the rule of clerical celibacy. By structural reform, I mean cultivating democratic modes at all levels. Celibate leadership arose in ages of monarchical and imperial power. The pope is king and his bishops are his vassals, even though they are supposed to be princes with some degree of autonomy. In this system, authority comes from God to the pope and his vicars. Vatican Council II developed a more democratic understanding of church as people of God, but it left the monarchical governance system intact. Since the sixties, the Vatican has increasingly centralized governance in the papacy. It is hard to give up power. The sentiments of the Medici Pope Leo X just before the Protestant Reformation still prevail: "God has given us the papacy, my brothers; let us enjoy it." Most celibate priests are not driven by power considerations. They serve people with dedication, wisdom and compassion. But I am talking about the basic infrastructure of the church, its mode of governance under which clergy and laity live.

Corrective movements to the accretion of power rose up at different historical moments. Individuals and groups endeavored to live closer to the spirit of Jesus, which stood against the power of empire. The early Jesus movement was constantly in tension with the dominant mentality of imperial Rome. This polarity shows up in the verse: "Render unto Caesar the things that are Caesar's and unto God the things that are God's." (Matthew 22:21) The contrast shows up in St. Francis's city of Assisi. Many tourists and religious pilgrims make their way to the imposing basilica that honors Francis and his order. The Franciscans were a reformist group seeking to live simple lives in an increasingly wealthy and powerful medieval church. Their mendicant ideals and actions tried to recapture the humbler ways of Jesus of Nazareth. The imposing upper basilica with its treasury of famous murals resembles an art museum. The lower crypt with its relics of Francis and his early companions offers a more meditative ambience.

A short drive into the hills above Assisi I found the *Eremo delle Carceri*, a hermitage where Francis went to contemplate the divine in nature. I experienced this place as an authentic environment of spiritual energy, away from the commercialism of the city and even the busy splendor of the basilica. The latter is in its own way a symbol of kingly power (*basileus*) that seems to entrap the free-spirited Francis in hierarchical control systems. But at the *Eremo delle Carceri* all this ecclesiastical folderol disappeared. There was the statue of Francis lying on his back amid plants contemplating the divine in stars, birds, and trees above him. The silence and rude simplicity spoke of genuineness, of the untrammeled still-point where oneness could prevail. My years of teaching ecology and religion sensitized me to the *Eremo*. I had spoken in class about Francis as an exemplar of Christian environmentalism over against so much otherworldliness and power-seeking in the Christian tradition.

Not long after this visit to Assisi, I had a similar experience in Washington's Sackler Gallery. I spent some time contemplating a Japanese print of Bodhidharma in the presence of Emperor Wu. The Buddhist missionary who brought his tradition to China would have understood Francis and felt kinship with him. Emperor Wu, who had been generous in helping nascent Buddhism in China, inquires about his reward for such munificence. Bodhidharma answers: "No merit." The emperor then asks him to define Buddhism. The monk replies: "Vast emptiness, nothing sacred." Finally, Wu asks who it is that kneels before him. "Don't know," says Bodhidharma. The first response reminds the emperor not to become attached to the outcomes of his desires. Francis, too, by his lifestyle was teaching the powerful to detach themselves from soul-destroying pomp and pride. "Vast emptiness, nothing sacred" might also define Francis's outlook. "Emptiness" in Buddhism means non-isolation of ego or anything else. In other words, everything is connected, and therefore, no one place is sacred because everything is sacred. At the *Eremo*, Francis finds the whole cosmos to be holy. He would have been embarrassed by the splendor of great churches in his honor. His embracing of poverty was a way of not maximizing the separate ego. Bodhidharma puts this experience of non-self succinctly, "don't know." Its hyperbole emphasizes the impermanence of all things, including the self-important self.

These reflections underline the direction of my spirituality as I approach my late seventies. I stay interested in the reform of religious institutions through reading and occasional writing. But I find myself more drawn to contemplative ways. I'm summoned by meditative practices that join wisdom from various traditions, including, of course, my Catholic Christianity. This spirituality has become more nature-oriented, ecumenical and metaphoric or parabolic, in the sense of parables that speak to deeper dimensions of life. As I mentioned earlier, New Testament scholar Marcus Borg has spoken cogently about such symbolic interpretations of religion over against literal ones. He points out how the true meaning of gospel stories lies in their metaphorical meaning. Does it matter, he asks, if the tale of the Good Samaritan or that of the Prodigal Son actually happened in history? What counts most is the parabolic meaning of these and many other parts of Scripture. I would extend this way of thinking to other religious doctrines in different traditions.

Such understanding undercuts much of the recent attack on religion by much publicized atheists (Richard Dawkins, Sam Harris, Christopher Hitchens). On one level, they rail against the abuses of institutional religion that are well known to most educated believers and scholars of religion. They tend to have blind spots for the positive contributions of religions. But the main point here is that the atheist attack focuses on a literalized, supernaturalist theism, a God understood as another entity, a being among beings, separate from the world but intervening in it. This narrows God down to a scapegoat figure who is driven from the scene by advances of science. These are naïve and limiting views of God, although they are still strong among less sophisticated religionists. But God must be spoken of metaphorically, mythically, by parable, by indirection, in poetry, art, and music. God is the greatest mystery, not in the sense of mystification, but in the way the *Tao Te Ching* opens: "The Tao that can be named is not the true Tao." Saints and mystics in all traditions express such views of the divine.

Sometimes I wonder if my approach is too inward and not social enough. From my earliest Jesuit days, I have been interested in the social gospel (in Catholic idiom, it was termed "social justice") and its later incarnations in liberation theology. Yet I haven't been an intense activist. I doubt that I have realized well the full interplay of resistance and contemplation, the title of a pacifist book by James Douglass. I've participated in my share of antiwar demonstrations from the Vietnam to the Iraqi wars. But I fall far behind colleagues and friends in committing a substantial part of my life to these endeavors. I follow world events with much interest and find myself a somewhat reconstructed liberal in later years. Some of my brother's conservatism has rubbed off on me, especially on the topic of personal responsibility over against forms of social engineering that contribute to the paralysis of self-victimization. I'm sure my social gospel proclivities are partially drawn from interpretations of Christianity and other religions. But I'm less bothered now about guilt for not being sufficiently involved in social change. Guilt about such things is not productive. Moreover, I have tried to make a social contribution through my teaching and writing. But elderhood brings with it a stronger sense of our limitations. An old Jesuit superior used to say, "Father, we are not divine providence." Amen to that. A more convincing answer to the inward-outward dilemma in terms of our spiritual energies comes from the contemplative side. We are invited to listen attentively to how the Spirit may be speaking from within. From that vantage point, we may act more wisely in the world.

For the last decade, I've felt the pull of artistic and literary inclinations. I've taken many courses in studio art and have tried my hand at watercolor, acrylics, and pastels. I've moved from amateur attempts at representational painting to abstraction. I've enjoyed doing an outdoor mural on my property in Athens. I took advantage of a large cement sewer (seven feet high by twelve feet around) near the Oconee River, which flows by my house. I painted a mural based on ancient Greek vases commemorating the annual Panathenaic celebration. I surrounded the singing and instrument-playing celebrants with plants and animals. This is capped by the sewer lid with the head of Pallas Athena in a large golden helmet. I enjoy seeing this early effort that has withstood floods and storms.

I also had a chance to act as impresario for a very large outdoor mural at Emory depicting the school's mission in colorful symbols. Much of my work was organizing and motivating others, but I did spend hours on ladders with brush in hand. I suppose that it's not unusual that the conceptual side of my brain, so to speak, with its religious studies background, would seek outlets from its right side. A number of my pieces express spiritual themes. Or that's what I tell myself. This new impetus in my life led me to open an art gallery for retired and active faculty exhibits in Emory's Emeritus College. Working on an art piece, while sometimes tedious and even disappointing, becomes a contemplative experience. My monkey mind seems to quiet down with full attention going to the work at hand. New insights about color or form pop up in the doing. It's a way of being pleasantly surprised by the products of one's own imagination, a symbol of staying open to grace.

My two novels are partially outcomes of spiritual interests. I hasten to add that I'm very aware of the pitfalls of turning a novel into a screed for ideas and making characters into vehicles for ideology. I struggled against this tendency to turn a novel into an essay. Yet I didn't want to dumb down fiction into action sound bites. I've tried to learn the craft of creative writing, steering between the Scylla of too much exposition and the Charybdis of mindless prose. I try to beat back the pedantic penchant by repeating to myself the contemporary mantra of "show me, don't tell me." But that, too, like all sacred slogans is overdone. Most American writers, giants like Melville, James, and Dreiser, would never have been published had they clung to that formula. A similar tension exists between the plot-based and the character-based novel, although a blend of both usually wins out. I've enjoyed the process of imagining forward both plot and character. Just as in pictorial art, surprises crop up while describing a scene or constructing a dialogue. This becomes the excitement of almost stumbling on a new possibility. Characters seem to take on minds of their own.

Both novels are about Catholics facing controversial issues and personal crises. After all, we were told to write about what we know. Mark Doyle, in *The Bishop of San Francisco*, is torn between his love for his therapist, Miriam Faberini, and his commitment to the church. Broader complications with the Vatican, as well as a right wing "death squad," intensify his conflict. I began writing this story about twenty years ago when I was staying in a Jesuit student residence in Florence. I was on leave from Emory, working on a project about natural religion as distinct from the supernaturalism that dominates much of Western religion. (My memoir is an extension of this perspective.) I decided that a novel could incorporate a movement toward a naturalist spirituality, a this-worldly religiousness. Thus Archbishop Mark Doyle became the protagonist of this story as he traveled from the sky religion of his youth to the earthiness of his political and romantic involvements. The challenge for a novice novelist was how to draw him away from ideology to be a flesh and blood human. The many versions of the novel over the years were attempts to learn the literary craft. I wanted to let wider themes emerge indirectly from the dramatic action.

My second novel, "*The Children's Crusade: Scandal at the Vatican,*" was more fun to do. I had gotten better at working plot, characters and dialogue. I wanted the book to be about the clerical abuse of children. As in the previous novel, I set out to combine personal struggle with institutional issues. The book starts with Dan Harrington, a college history professor who had been molested by his parish priest, and it ends with Pope Clement XV struggling with a momentous decision concerning accusations of child abuse from an earlier period of his life. Bishop Mark Doyle is again drawn into the action when he sides with critics of the Vatican over cover-ups. Doyle, the father of a love child, faces more tensions with his lover. Sr. Frankie Latrobe, an African-American nun, becomes romantically involved with Harrington as they follow clues that lead to the papal office. Frankie gradually helps Dan overcome some inner problems stemming from his own child abuse. The novel indirectly drives home the issue of hierarchical accountability for the many cover-ups.

This late-life journey into art and fiction brings me back to the shifting territory of my own self-understanding. Painting and novel-writing are ways of making and remaking reality. Our lives have some relatively stable aspects like our genetic component and our continuous memory of ourselves. But our thoughts and experiences are also constantly changing. Here I think again of the title of Whitehead's lectures, *Religion in the Making*, that pinpoints change. This is true not only for religious institutions, but also for one's inner life. *Homo faber*, man the maker, is an essential part of who we are as we shape culture. On the personal level, we are forever "selving," as Gerald Manley Hopkins noted.

Yet our "selving" always happens in community. We are made in large part through our interaction with others. I reflect on this a good deal in my late seventies. I thought about it especially while writing the last section of this memoir as I walked through the neighborhood where I grew up in Oakland. The theme of Proust's famous book came to mind, the search into times gone by. I remembered the crucial support of family, school, and community. I saw the faces and heard the voices of these early actors. I also sensed the inadequacies of all our encounters. As I walked through the old streets, I was of two minds. I was grateful that my family did the best it could for me, and I was saddened that we didn't understand each other as well as we might have. As I walked through my old district, specific memories inspired this poem:

> Steam engine wheezes and chugs
> like a bear pawing the ground
> ready to charge—all aboard!
> I hold the Italian Catholic Federation banner
> while *Barba Gianni* cradles his clarinet
> at the Santa Fe station
> now swallowed by this Starbucks and Home Depot.
> Like Proust I pursue lost times
> holding *Nonna's* hand walking Adeline Street
> echoes of the mission preacher resounding *Noi vogliam Dio*
> as we pick mushrooms and eucalyptus pods
> in lots now gone condo without mercy.
> I crouch in a trench for the great grassball war
> missiles sailing overhead (Ma calling to dinner)
> in a vast field on 42nd Street
> now a nondescript factory sprouting cantina wire.
> I visit *Nonno* watering rows of Swiss chard
> with tin pail at the end of a long pole.
> We sit by the iron well pump
> as he reveals secrets hidden from the beginning of the world.
> Pushing back white hair, I see his garden covered
> by ugly box apartments from the fifties.
> Such memories surge virtual
> but real enough to console.
>   —"Seventy Years Later"

   This dual feeling of thanksgiving and disappointment runs through all my closest relationships, from family to friends to former wives. By a happier alchemy, Peggy and I over two decades have been able to come closer, to contribute to our mutual "selving." But this, too, is a work in progress, that requires daily self-assessment and mutual listening. My poem written for our tenth wedding anniversary captures some of the concreteness of our home in Athens linked to my feelings for Peggy:

> You have become many presences to me.
> You are the Oconee struggling through drought,
> flowing with life for heron and hawk,
> swelling on flood tide to soak forgotten roots on high ground.
> You are the velvet crow squawking in the oak tree,
> bird of persistence,
> knowing right from wrong,
> just from unjust,
> swooping like mockingbird to guard sacred grounds.
> You are the house-home built with dearest care,
> friendly hands linked to yours;
> you have raised its rafters like the tent of Yahweh,
> a hovering kindness over the wayfarer.
> You are cat and dog,
> speaking the rare lingo of Siamese puma-dude and spacey poodle
> playing and mothering,
> mammal to mammal.
> You are garden of stone and flower,
> caressing the names of all sprouting things,
> like Eve in Eden,
> greeting their coming with child delight,
> cheering on the moss and the peony.
> You are the distant cell phone,
> moving fatigued across the Georgia night
> after massaging contentious egos . . .
> to make sure the old guy, back from his harem,
> is tucked in with a virtual kiss.
> You are the wordless presence in a thousand places
> that slides silently across my soul,
> bride of my body, echo of love.
>
> —"Peggy"

The way of listening seems a good note on which to end this chapter. I began it with the idea of staying open to one's *intention profonde*, one's deeper self or Self, not the clamor of ego desires. I think this is what Hopkins meant by "selving." In Christian language it signifies attention to the quiet urgings of the Spirit who is one with us. To really listen to the pulse of Spirit-life in and around us, we need to cultivate silence and stillness. My life has been very active. I don't regret that because there has been much pleasure in my involvements as teacher, writer and, perhaps, religious reformer. But since I have put so much energy into the topic of creative aging, I can hardly avoid one of its key lessons, slowing down enough in the shortened time ahead to wake up and listen to deeper promptings. This doesn't mean withdrawal from life, but it requires more time in the hermitage above Assisi with Francis or in the cave at Manresa with Ignatius. It calls for the not-knowing of Bodhidharma before Emperor Wu and of Lao Tse throughout the *Tao Te Ching*.

This listening posture is one of not-knowing in the presence of mystery. I'm especially drawn to the nature mysticism of Francis and of the Tao masters. This seems to accord with the environmental crisis around us. Or to put it in New Testament terms, I'd like to be among the vigilant virgins when the bridegroom returns. This means that I don't want to be mesmerized by actions, even worthy ones, that accompany the gift of good health. Or to put it in Jesuit language, to be a contemplative in action denotes a doing that is suffused with silent listening, a way of prayer.

2005: At home on the Oconee River

Epilogue

Listening to the Cicadas

The world is God's language to us.

—SIMONE WEIL

As GUESTS OF THE University of Toulouse a few years ago, Peggy and I had a chance to explore parts of southern France. One of our sojourns was to Montsegur near the Pyrenees where the medieval Cathars held out against the crusaders of the Pope and the French king. Montsegur, a fortress town on the peak of a mountain, was something of a Cathar Masada. When it fell in 1244, the crusaders burned to death all the survivors of the siege, over two hundred people. The Cathar or Albigensian heresy provoked the first inquisition led by the new order of Dominicans. I wanted to visit the ruins as a pilgrimage of repentance for still another act of violence in the name of religion. I figured that the Pope would be too busy to make the trip for himself. Peggy wasn't up for the climb so she waited in the village below. The day was probably too cool and foggy for tourists, so I had the old stones to myself after a steep ascent. I stayed so long that Peggy was about to send gendarmes to the rescue. Memories of that solo hike seem to fit the writing of a memoir. I had to find my own way up the mountain after leaving the settled world below. It was a journey into less known terrain.

Sitting on a medieval staircase, I meditated on religion linked to intolerance, political power, and the quest for wealth. The Languedoc region was among the most prosperous areas of France in the early thirteenth century. I imagined the terror of those herded together as the flames mounted. While I didn't share the Cathars' view about the world as evil, I admired their communal virtues and their opposition to the union of church and crown. Had I lived back then with the tenets I hold now, I would have been a good candidate for exclusion and even execution. My afternoon among the gray remnants of Montsegur made me ponder how best to live the rest of my life and face my own death.

My only personal certainty about the time to come is my own demise. I'm in good health now, but I know that the road ahead isn't long. As a reader of obituaries, I see that people don't live much beyond their seventies or eighties. I know all this intellectually, but it's still hard to imagine my own end in an experiential way. Many friends are already gone. Since I can't be truly realistic about my own passing, the best I can do is to reflect on how I'd like to live in the interim. If I can shape an inner life for the final season, I may be ready to realize Teilhard de Chardin's injunction to "*finir bien.*"

Anxieties about my death are not so clear that I can list them in order. They exist as an undercurrent of life that wells up in special circumstances. Some tell me that they have no fear of death. My psychologist side wants to say they are in denial. But such people may be right about themselves. Maybe their brain chemistry precludes death anxieties. Geneticists may one day find the don't-worry gene. However that may be, I don't expect to go with quiet heroism "into that good night." But if my blood pressure spikes in a doctor's office are any indication, I will not be fear-free during a protracted dying.

There was a time when I thought such weakness showed a lack of inner strength. But I don't believe that now. The earlier view was driven by a superhuman ideal, a form of Platonic perfection. It was going up into a sky of unreachable and crippling images. We saw God as absolute good. We weren't supposed to be God, of course, but we were to strive in that direction. Now I view God as an ever-widening mystery, something like the expanding universe. Yet within my agnostic grasp of this transcendence, I sense God as an immanence quietly embracing all the sufferings and joys of my existence. While I want to live out my days in just and caring ways, I accept my shortcomings and fears as my own oddball friends.

Acceptance in face of death opens possibilities for embracing myself as I am in every moment. This doesn't mean excusing myself for mistreating others or disregarding their needs. I hope to do less of that, but I know I will fall short. I will have to ask forgiveness of others and forgive myself. This is an inevitable pattern of life. In this regard, a sense of humor toward oneself is a great antidote to excessive self-absorption.

An intentional contemplative life also helps toward self-acceptance. In meditation we back up from our preoccupations and see them in perspective. Contemplation lets us view all this from a quiet place. This leads to detachment, not from the world and its needs, but from the outcomes of our excessive desires. We become freer to enjoy and contribute to what is. In Christian terms, it opens us to more loving ways. In Buddhist language, we are freer to be compassionate. Finally, the contemplative way brings us into a wordless presence where Spirit can transform us. That is the calming still point where we are at peace, accepting and accepted.

Reflection on the contemplative brings me back to my discussion of saints and sanctity in the Introduction. This overview of my life confirms an imperfect yet truer view of sanctity or wholeness. I hope it places the saint beyond the confines of ecclesiastical descriptions. We then see holiness in all creation. If sanctity is ultimately about wholeness, it is also very much about making our peace with our un-wholeness, with an unconditional acceptance of ourselves as we are. It even calls for celebrating that un-wholeness.

In earlier talks about creative aging, I used to end up with the vision of making a complete mosaic of life. I don't do that anymore. I then had in mind the marvelous mosaics that grace the vaults of European churches, many of Christ and Mary, others of important folk like Theodosius and his court in Ravenna. I talked about many pieces of a life coming together to shape the completed image. Now I realize that those ideal mosaics were extraordinary art, but not real replicas of lives lived. I think this is true for all humans from Jesus to the humblest among us. This, of course, is not a plea for mediocrity or a way of justifying the unethical. Rather contemplative practice helps us focus on the imperfect now, that kaleidoscope of happenings where we listen for the Spirit breaking through.

I've discovered certain virtues that I'd like to cultivate in late life. For these insights I thank the many elders I've studied in research on aging. The first is gratitude. To age in a spirit of thankfulness guards against resentment. The pull of resentment is always there. If only this or that hadn't happened, I would have had a better life. It's the "if only" syndrome. Dag Hammarskjöld sums up the antidote to resentment: "For all that has been, Thanks! To all that shall be, Yes!" (*Markings*)

Another trait of creative aging is forgiveness. This doesn't amount to excusing or forgetting offenses. It means forgiving my own dark side. And it involves forgiving those who have hurt us. Without this quality, we carry bitterness that affects body and mind.

Aging well also calls for an attitude of celebration. I cherish this trait because I haven't done enough of it in a life driven by attaining goals. We can celebrate beauty in its small and large manifestations. It presupposes slowing down to experience the present.

Spiritual aging summons us to face our diminishments, the small deaths, physical and mental. Some of us experience physical decline in defined ways, such as serious breakdowns of vision, hearing or mobility. Other impairments of the elderly are diabetes, heart disease, and cancer. We generally experience a decline in energy. I notice how the young walk faster than I do. Then there are the psychological losses from the deaths of friends and family to the loss of status through retirement. In my late seventies, I'm more frequently aware of such diminishments. Carl Jung spoke of the possibility of spiritual ascent in the midst of these physical/psychological declines. But for this contretemps to work, we need to be open to inward and outward spiritual resources.

Letting go gracefully summarizes spirit life in the context of our diminishments. It involves relinquishing old scripts and less creative desires. In this process, we become lamps unto ourselves, as the Buddha advised. But to live this way, we must improvise. We can't write the libretto ahead of time. Like jazz artists, we learn piecemeal how to adapt to new events. Letting go gracefully is not a passive exercise. We need to be actively aware of the promptings of grace that arise with every loss and transition. It calls for being mindful in the moment.

I also want to cultivate external resources that can enhance spiritual aging. Although I use the word "external," these outward blessings are intimately linked to inner life. I'm thinking about the importance of friends, old and new. Friendship is such sustaining joy and a mutual source of support. My marriage is a primary friendship among others. Life with Peggy for the past twenty years has been central to my finding a spiritual home. As complex people, we encounter the usual frustrations of life together. Yet the core of our marital friendship rests on mutual respect and caring.

We walk the path together. But as Anne Morrow Lindbergh said, the mature husband and wife face outward together. So the spiritual process circles outward toward wider communities. We continue to grapple with the messy world of politics, war and injustice. We look for places to be of service, even in small ways. Our spiritual community extends to the world of nature. Peggy has created a wonderful garden and we share life with our animal companions, now two cats. I am much more conscious of myself as part of the vast natural world.

Yet to talk about our planet as a whole is too distant and conceptual. In more immediate ways, ecology comes home to me when I work in our garden. I have experienced the planet as a whole only from afar in pictures from space. Now I have my feet on the ground as I sit on a bench behind my home looking out on the Oconee River. On one side I see the memorial garden my wife and I built. It is a simple circle of stones and low-lying plants with a Japanese maple in the center. Some of the ashes of our animals and of Peggy's mother will be buried there. In the normal course of things some of my ashes will also rest there. This gives me a special sense of place, of home. These are the dog days of August. Heavy humidity seems to melt me into the plants and trees that are trying to hold their own in a long drought. I've thought of my breath connecting me to nature, but never my sweat. Yet this perspiration is part of the connection pointing to an encircling unity beyond our divisions.

My feet are not resting on the dark, hard-packed loam of the Oakland flatlands in my grandfather's basement where old Italians were making red wine in 1938. But I see this red clay of Georgia as a continuous membrane of soil covering the curving horizon of time and space. The eight-year-old boy in Oakland wouldn't have had an inkling that his feet would end up in Georgia seven decades later. He wouldn't have had a clue about the medieval thinkers' understanding of *ricorso*, the return of all things to their source. He had yet to read T.S. Eliot, who spoke about each of us finding the place where we began and recognizing it in depth for the first time. The boy knew nothing about a sojourn from sky to earth religion, or of the presence of the transcendent within the immanent . . . right under his feet. I look at the same feet, more or less. I haven't always kept them wisely on the ground, nor have I always walked the right path in relationships. But even in this, at some deeper place, we can forgive one another.

With respect for ancient monastic tradition, we Jesuit novices observed the nightly great silence. It was called *magnum silentium* with the Latin lending it a cachet of gravitas. Tonight I will come back to this bench that I rebuilt to sit and listen to what I'd call the great sound. Silence and stillness have wonderful uses, but so does sound, reaching from the Big Bang to tonight's concert by the moonlit Oconee River. When I hear the thunderous song of the cicadas, I will remember the story of the spiritual master instructing his disciples:

> When the disciples asked for a model
> Of spirituality that they could imitate,
> All that the master said was: "Hush! Listen,"
> And as they listened to the sounds
> of the night outside the monastery,
> the master softly intoned the
> celebrated haiku:
>> *"Of an early death*
>> *showing no awareness*
>> *the cicada sings."*
>> —FROM *ONE MINUTE WISDOM* BY ANTHONY DE MELLO.